Jonathan Swift

Gulliver's Travels

Adaptation and activities
by **Derek Sellen**
Illustrated by **Franco Rivolli**

Member of CISQ Federation

CERTIFIED MANAGEMENT SYSTEM
ISO 9001

The design, production and distribution of educational materials for the CIDEB (Black Cat) brand are managed in compliance with the rules of Quality Management System which fulfils the requirements of the standard ISO 9001

Content editor: Maria Grazia Donati
Editor: Emma Berridge
Design: Sara Fabbri, Erika Barabino
Page Layout: Annalisa Possenti
Picture research: Alice Graziotin

Art Director: Nadia Maestri

© 2017 Black Cat
First edition: February 2017

DEALINK, DEAFLIX are trademarks licensed by De Agostini SpA

Picture credits:
Shutterstock; iStockphoto; Dreamstime; Science Photo Library/AGF:4; De Agostini Picture Library: 5,76,78; Mary Evans/AGF: 72; WebPhoto: 74,75.

All rights reserved. No part of this book may be reproduced, stored in a retrieval system or transmitted, in any form or by any means, electronic, mechanical, photocopying, recording or otherwise, without the written permission of the publisher.

We would be happy to give you further information concerning our material and receive your comments.

info@blackcat-cideb.com
blackcat-cideb.com

Printed in Italy by Litoprint, Genoa

Contents

4 ▶ About Jonathan Swift

8 ▶ Before you read

Chapter 1
In Lilliput   10

Chapter 2
Making Friends   16

Chapter 3
War and Fire   22

Chapter 4
Goodbye, Lilliput   28

Chapter 5
The Land of the Giants   35

Chapter 6
Entertaining the Giants   41

Chapter 7
A Dangerous Life   45

Chapter 8
The Flying Island   52

Chapter 9
The Land of Ghosts   59

Chapter 10
The Land of Wise Horses   64

72 ▶ **Dossiers** Popular travel books
Gulliver's Travels on screen   74
Utopia and Dystopia   76

79 ▶ **Activities**

n.track   THE STORY IS FULLY RECORDED

About Jonathan Swift

Jonathan Swift was born in 1667 in Dublin. He was educated at Kilkenny Grammar School, and then Trinity College Dublin. After leaving university he worked as secretary to Sir William Temple, and became involved in political life.

Swift was unhappy at the direction his career was taking, and he became a minister of the Church in 1694. He continued to take part in political debate through his writing. He made many enemies through his satires on political and religious life. In one famous essay he suggested that poverty in Ireland could be reduced by eating the babies of the poor!

There are many well-known quotations from Swift's books, letters and conversations. Here are a few:

'We have just enough religion to make us hate, but not enough to make us love one another.' = Religion can cause wars and hatred; but true religion causes us to love one another.

'One enemy can do more hurt than ten friends can do good.'

'The best doctors in the world are Doctor Diet, Doctor Quiet, and Doctor Merryman.' = You will have good health if you eat healthily, have a calm life and are happy.

He had two important friendships with women during his life. He met Esther Johnson in 1689 when she was a child and later they exchanged a famous series of letters. He called her 'Stella' and it is possible that he married her in 1716 although this is uncertain. He met another important female friend, Esther Vanhomrigh, in 1707 and gave her the nickname[1] of 'Vanessa', a name which he invented.

In 1713 Swift became Dean[2] of St. Patrick's in Dublin. He was a very popular figure in Ireland, and supported local charities very generously. His behaviour was increasingly strange in the last years of his life, and many people believed that he was mad. Swift died in 1745.

Swift's reputation suffered in the 18th and 19th centuries, as critics thought his work was too angry and vulgar. During the 20th century, however, his work was admired by critics, and his reputation is now very high. His most famous books include: *The Battle of the Books* (1704), *A Tale of a Tub* (1704) and *Gulliver's Travels* (1726).

---

1. **nickname:** unofficial name, given to you by friends or family.
2. **Dean :** important priest in the Roman Catholic Church.

▶ **Gulliver** wakes up in Lilliput by Arthur Rackham (1909).

1 Look at the sentences below. Decide if each statement is correct or incorrect. If it is correct, mark A. If it is not correct, mark B.

                                                                              A B

1. Jonathan Swift was born in London in 1667.
2. He studied at university in Dublin.
3. He became a minister of the Church in 1694.
4. In one famous essay he suggested that poverty in Ireland could be reduced if rich people ate poor people.
5. He was unpopular in Ireland.
6. He died in 1755.
7. Modern critics do not like Jonathan Swift's work because they think it is too angry and vulgar.

2 Here are some more quotations from Swift. Use words from the box to complete the explanations.

> admit   emotions   good   help   lazy   powerful   shouldn't   wrong

1. *I never knew a man come to greatness or eminence who lay abed late in the morning.*
   = People who are .... never become important or ....
2. *Blessed is he who expects nothing, for he shall never be disappointed.*
   People who do not expect .... things in their lives will not be disappointed.
3. *Power is no blessing in itself, except when it is used to protect the innocent.*
   = Power is only useful when you can use it to .... innocent people.
4. *A wise man should have money in his head, but not in his heart.*
   = Money is important but you .... let it influence your ....
5. *There are few, very few, that will own themselves in a mistake.*
   Few people like to .... that they are ....

The Characters

Top row, from left to right: a Houyhnhnm, a Yahoo, the Emperor of Lilliput
Second row, from left to right: the Queen of Brobdingnag, Glumdalclitch, Lemuel Gulliver

BEFORE YOU READ

1 Vocabulary • Look at these 16 items of vocabulary. Use a dictionary to check any unfamiliar words. Then match the words in pairs by linking similar items together. There is an example.

1. [12] accident at sea
2. [ ] procession
3. [ ] die in the water
4. [ ] voyage
5. [ ] journey by sea
6. [ ] kingdom
7. [ ] take prisoner
8. [ ] palace

9. [ ] parade
10. [ ] capture
11. [ ] royal building
12. [ ] shipwreck
13. [ ] storm
14. [ ] nation
15. [ ] very bad weather
16. [ ] drown

2 Plot • Gulliver visits many different lands. Look at some of the things which the inhabitants of these lands do during the story. Match the countries to the events by writing letters in the spaces. As you go on to read *Gulliver's Travels*, see if you guessed correctly.

1. [ ] A land of little people
2. [ ] A land of giants
3. [ ] A land of professors
4. [ ] A land of magicians
5. [ ] A land of people who never die
6. [ ] A land of intelligent horses

a   They carry Gulliver from place to place in a special box.
b   They lose their memories and become very weak.
c   They have a rational society which is based on friendship and truth.
d   They have crazy theories which have negative results.
e   They are afraid of Gulliver and tie him up so he cannot move.
f   They make people appear and disappear.

3 Satire • Satire is a kind of comedy where the author uses a story to laugh at things in society. Below there are six subjects which Swift satirises in the story. There are also six events which help him to satirise them. Match 1-6 with a-f.

1. ☐ war   2. ☐ universities and over-education   3. ☐ our idea of a hero
4. ☐ politics   5. ☐ monarchy   6. ☐ human society

a The ghosts of famous people are in fact cruel and stupid.
b Two nations fight for a ridiculous reason.
c People do stupid things in order to get government jobs.
d The Yahoos, who are dirty and violent, remind Gulliver of people in England.
e An Emperor changes from a friend to an enemy without a good reason.
f Professors give stupid advice to farmers.

4 Gulliver and you! • Look at a-h. Some are reasons to feel sorry for Gulliver and some are reasons to admire him. Write the letters in the appropriate part of the table. There is an example.

a Gulliver often has accidents on his voyages.
b He is brave and rarely afraid.
c He finds clever solutions to problems.
d The people he meets often treat him badly.
e He is often separated from his own family and friends.
f He loves adventure.
g He refuses to use his strength to make war against some little people.
h He often meets stupid or untrustworthy people.

Reasons to feel sorry for Gulliver	Reasons to admire Gulliver
a	

As you read the story, ask yourself how you feel about Gulliver.

CHAPTER 1

In Lilliput

Let me introduce myself. I am Lemuel Gulliver and this is the story of my voyages. I was born in England in 16--. After I had finished my studies in medicine, I worked in London. However, it was difficult to make money there. I liked travelling and I wanted to have an interesting life, so I decided to become a ship's doctor.

One ship I worked on was called the *Antelope*. Our voyage went very well at first, but one day there was a great storm. The ship hit a rock in the sea, and began to sink. I managed to jump into one of the ship's lifeboats[1] with some sailors, and we thought we were safe. Then there was a big wave, and the little boat turned over in the water. We all began to swim. I soon lost sight of the other sailors, and I never saw them again. I think they all drowned.

---

1. **lifeboat :** boat used to save people when a ship sinks.

In Lilliput

I swam for many hours in the water, and I was very tired. Suddenly I realised that the water was not deep any more – my feet touched the ground! I walked a long time, and then I came to the beach. It was evening, and I was exhausted. I fell asleep on the sand.

When I woke up it was morning. I tried to stand up, but I could not move at all. I raised my head a little, and I could see ropes [2] around my body. They were tied very tightly.[3] I did not know what had happened to me.

Then I saw a very small creature walking along my body. I looked again, and I was very surprised to see that this creature was really a tiny man! Soon there were more of these little men walking on me. There were hundreds of them on the ground near me. They were talking to each other, but I could not understand their language.

I shouted very loudly, and the little men were afraid. They ran away quickly. Then I tried to free myself, and I managed to break the ropes around one of my hands. As soon as I did this, I felt a sharp pain. The little men were shooting arrows [4] at me! The arrows were very small, but they were also very sharp, and I decided to lie still.[5]

Now the little men constructed a platform near my head. One of them climbed up to the top of the platform. He was standing very close to my ear. He began to shout into my ear. I could hear what he said, but I did not understand the language he was using. He used signs to communicate with me. He told me that the country was called Lilliput, and that he worked for the Emperor. Then he

---

2. **rope :**
3. **tightly :** firmly.
4. **arrow :**
5. **still :** without moving.

CHAPTER 1

explained that I was their prisoner. He told me not to be frightened, because they only wanted to take me to see the Emperor.

It was now the middle of the morning, and I was hungry and thirsty. I put my finger in my mouth to show the little man that I wanted to eat and drink something. He understood me, and he gave some instructions to the hundreds of little men who were on the ground. They went away, and then they came back with ladders. They had wine and food with them. They climbed up the ladders, and offered me the wine and food. Everything tasted good, but it was very small, like the men themselves. I drank whole barrels [6] of wine, and ate several cows and sheep.

Soon I could hear a lot of noise on the ground near me. I turned my head to look, and I saw that all the little men were now very busy. They had cut down a lot of trees, and they were building something with the trees. They worked for a long time, and then I saw what they were making. It was a large machine with many wheels. The machine was as big as me.

I was now tired again, and I fell asleep once more. While I slept, the little men pulled me onto the machine. The movement woke me. I was curious to find out what they were doing.

Then I heard a noise, and I saw hundreds of tiny horses. The little men attached the horses to the machine, and the horses began to pull me along. There were fifteen hundred horses pulling me! The machine began to move slowly forward.

We travelled slowly for a long time, and then we came to a city. We stopped outside the city. There was a very old temple here, and they asked me to get off the machine and enter the temple. I learned later that this temple was one of the largest buildings in the country. It was no longer used because someone had committed a terrible murder [7] there some years before. There was just enough space in

---

6. **barrel :** wooden container for liquids.
7. **murder :** when one person kills another person.

the temple for me to enter. Once I was inside, the people tied me up again. They used ninety-one chains and thirty-six locks! The chains were long enough to allow me to stand and walk around. I'll never forget how surprised and frightened the people were, when they saw me stand up and walk!

Now the Emperor himself came to the temple. He brought his princess with him. They wanted to look at me. They climbed up a tower in the temple, and looked down at me where I lay. People from the city began to arrive as well, and they climbed up the walls of the temple to look down at me. Some very daring[8] people put ladders against my body, and climbed up these. Everybody was very surprised to see me. I was the biggest man they had ever seen!

---

8. daring : brave, courageous.

THINK!

Look at the list of values and feelings below. Think of situations from Chapter 1 where these values and feelings are part of the story.

bravery   strength   fear   curiosity   creativity   surprise   disbelief

For example:

bravery: *Gulliver swims for many hours in the sea.*
The Lilliputians approach Gulliver although he seems like a giant.

The text and beyond • page 80
Values & Feelings • page 110

CHAPTER 2

Making Friends

It was difficult to communicate with the people of Lilliput. The Emperor came to see me again but he did not understand English. I tried other languages but he knew none of them. After about two hours, he went away. He ordered some soldiers to guard me.

Some of the people from the city began to come near me. They, too, wanted to see the giant man. Not all of them were friendly, however. A small group of them began to shoot arrows at me. The colonel in charge of the soldiers was very angry, and he captured six of the ringleaders.[1] He told the soldiers to tie them with ropes. Then he gave them to me to punish. I picked up all six men in my hand, and put five of them into my pocket. I lifted the sixth man very close to my face. I pretended that I wanted to eat him, and took out

---

1. **ringleader** : person responsible for bad behaviour.

Making Friends

my penknife.[2] The colonel and the soldiers looked unhappy when they saw me doing this – and the prisoner was terrified! I put the knife near the man's body, and gently cut the ropes around him. Then I placed him on the ground. I did the same thing with the other five men. The soldiers and the people were very happy when they saw that I was kind to the men who had tried to hurt me with their arrows.

The Emperor asked his government ministers what to do with me. They suggested that someone should teach me their language. I studied very hard, and in about a month I could speak it. Then I told the Emperor that I was tired of being a prisoner. I asked him to let me go. He said that he would consider my request. He asked me to be patient, and he told me they would treat me well.

Then the Emperor told me that he wanted his soldiers to search me for weapons. I replied that I would show his men everything I had in my pockets. The Emperor thanked me, but he explained that the law was very clear: the search had to be carried out by the Emperor's men themselves. He asked me to help the men carry out the search. I agreed to do this. I picked up the two men very carefully, and put them into my coat pockets. The two men later wrote a report for the Emperor. This is what they said in the report:

We found a very large piece of cloth in the giant's right pocket. In his left pocket we found a very large metal box. We asked the giant man to open this box for us. It contained a kind of powder that made us sneeze[3] a lot. Then we looked in the giant's right waistcoat-pocket.[4] We found some pieces of white material, and

2. **penknife :**

3. **sneeze :**

4. **waistcoat-pocket :** pocket of a small sleeveless jacket.

CHAPTER 2

these were tied with ropes. We think these are papers, because there seems to be writing on them. The letters are very large – each letter is as big as a man's hand! We found a huge machine in the giant's left waistcoat-pocket. This machine has about twenty pieces of metal on it. We think it is the giant's comb.[5] In both of his trouser pockets we found a very long tube of metal attached to a piece of wood. We do not know what this is. Then we saw a very large chain that went into another pocket. We asked the giant to show us the whole chain. He pulled it out of his pocket, and we saw a large machine on the end of it. The machine is round, and it has writing on it. This machine makes a huge noise. We do not know if the machine is an animal, or a kind of god. We believe it may be the giant's god, because of something he told us. He said,

'I never do anything without looking at this first.'

The giant has a belt around his body, and there are some objects hanging from this. We saw a huge sword,[6] the length of five men. We also saw a large bag on the belt. This contains some metal balls and some black powder – we do not know what these are.

I did not show the two men the pocket where I kept my glasses.

The Emperor was very curious to see all the objects described in the report. First he asked to see my sword. Then he wanted to see the 'very long tube of metal attached to a piece of wood.' I explained that this was my pistol, and I offered to fire it for him. I took some of the 'black powder', and put it into the pistol. Then I fired – the noise frightened the Emperor's soldiers very much! Next the Emperor wanted to see my watch. He did not know what it was, but he was very interested in the noise it made.

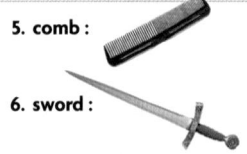

5. comb :

6. sword :

CHAPTER 2

Everybody in Lilliput was very happy with my behaviour, and the people began to trust me. Sometimes they came to dance on my hand. The children played hide and seek[7] in my hair.

The Emperor was very pleased with me as well, and he invited me to see some special dances. These dances are performed in the Emperor's court, by his ministers and other important people. They are very strange dances. For the first dance, they place a rope above the ground, and the ministers dance on this rope. The government minister who does the best dance is given a government job. These dances are very dangerous, and there are many accidents. Most of the Emperor's ministers fall off the rope sooner or later, and are injured.

There is another kind of dance that is performed in the Emperor's court. This dance is performed for the Emperor, the Empress, and the first minister. The Emperor puts some coloured threads[8] on a table. The threads are blue, red, and green. Then the dancers enter the room, and the performance begins. The Emperor holds a long piece of wood in front of himself. The dancers jump over the wood, or go under it. The Emperor raises and lowers the wood all the time, and it is difficult for the dancers to know whether they have to jump or to go under the wood. The best dancer is given the blue thread, the second best dancer is given the red one, and the third best is given the green one. Everyone in the court wants to win a blue thread. It is a great honour to have a piece of blue thread.

7. **hide and seek :** game of pursuit played by children.
8. **thread :** fibre such as cotton.

Making Friends

I thought it was a good idea to make a friend of the Emperor, and I tried to please him. He was very proud of his soldiers, and this gave me an idea. One day I organised a special military parade for him. I placed some sticks on the ground. Then I tied my handkerchief to the sticks, and lifted some of the Emperor's horsemen onto the handkerchief. They had a parade in the air, and this amused the Emperor greatly! Another time, the Emperor's army had a parade near the city. The Emperor asked me to stand very still with my feet apart, and the whole army marched [9] between my legs!

I asked the Emperor again to give me my freedom. The Emperor asked his ministers if this was a good idea. They said I had to agree to certain conditions before I could have my freedom. The two most important conditions were these: I must not leave Lilliput without permission, and I must help the Emperor's army if there was a war. I agreed to these conditions, and the Emperor gave me my freedom.

---

9. march : walk in procession.

THINK!

Swift laughs at customs and beliefs in the real world by writing about Lilliput. Match 1-5 with a-d.

Swift describes:	He is criticising:
1. ☐ The best dancers are chosen for government jobs.	**a** Complicated military parades.
2. ☐ People dance and receive different-coloured threads.	**b** Kings who love power and glory.
3. ☐ The Emperor is very proud of his soldiers.	**c** Ambitious politicians.
4. ☐ The army marches between Gulliver's legs.	**d** Medals and other honours given by kings.

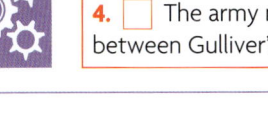

> **The text and beyond** • page 82
> **Values & Feelings** • page 110

CHAPTER 3

War and Fire

I was able to help the Emperor on two occasions but it wasn't simple. It all began when I visited the capital city, which is called Mildendo. The Emperor had given me permission to go there. 'Be careful when you are there. Do not frighten the people,' he told me. I liked the city very much. The most important building is the Emperor's palace. I was too big to go inside but when I looked through the windows, I saw that it was very beautiful.

I stayed in Mildendo about two weeks. One of the Emperor's ministers came to see me one day. He looked very worried, and he said he needed my help. Then he told me that there was going to be a war with the country of Blefuscu. He explained the reasons for the war. They seemed very strange reasons to me, because they concerned[1] the correct way to eat eggs. In the past, the people of

---

1. concerned : involved, regarded.

War and Fire

Lilliput and the people of Blefuscu had agreed about this. They had both believed that eggs should be broken at the bigger end.

One day, however, the Emperor's grandfather had an accident while he was opening an egg. He cut his finger. He ordered all Lilliputians to open eggs from the smaller end in the future. The people did not like this order, and many of them refused to obey the Emperor. There was a civil war in Lilliput, and many people were killed. The Emperor's minister explained to me that Blefuscu supported the rebels in the civil war – many rebels went to live in Blefuscu.

The situation was now very serious because Lilliput and Blefuscu were at war. Thousands of people had been killed in the war of the eggs. The government minister told me that Blefuscu was planning to attack Lilliput. The Emperor wanted my help. I told the minister that I was ready to help the Emperor.

The Blefuscu navy was planning to invade Lilliput by sea. The distance between the two countries is about three hundred metres by sea. All the Blefuscu ships were ready, and they were sure they would be victorious in the war. I told the Emperor of Lilliput that I had a plan of my own to help him defeat the enemy.

I waited until it was dark. Then I took some rope with me, and walked into the sea that separated the two kingdoms. The water was not deep. While I was walking in the sea, I put on my glasses to protect my eyes from the arrows of the enemy. I tied a piece of rope to each of the Blefuscu ships. The Blefuscu sailors were terrified when they saw me. They jumped into the sea, and swam away. I took the pieces of rope in my hands, and pulled the Blefuscu navy towards Lilliput.

When the people of Lilliput saw the Blefuscu navy, they thought the invasion had started. They were very frightened now!

Then they saw that I was pulling the ships, and they were happy. It was a great victory for Lilliput, and the Emperor said I was a hero.

War and Fire

The Emperor of Lilliput asked me to go on with the war against Blefuscu. I did not want to go on with the war, because I did not want lots of people to be killed. The Emperor listened to what I said, but he was very angry with me. Now he did not like me.

Some government ministers from Blefuscu came to Lilliput. I spoke to them, and they invited me to visit their country. I thanked them for their invitation, and I decided to ask the Emperor for permission to go there.

'The Blefuscu ministers have asked me to visit their country,' I told him. 'May I go there?'

The Emperor looked at me very coldly before he replied. Then he said,

'Of course. You're free to go.'

I was surprised at the Emperor's coldness towards me, because I thought we were good friends. Soon I had an opportunity to help him once again. One night I was woken by a great noise in the city. Many people were shouting and calling for me. Several of the government ministers came to me, and they told me there was a fire in the

CHAPTER 3

palace. I ran to the palace, and I saw flames everywhere. People were trying to extinguish [2] the flames with buckets of water – but the fire was a big one. It seemed that the whole palace would be destroyed. Then I had an idea. I had drunk a large quantity of wine that evening. I urinated over the palace, and extinguished the flames. This act saved the palace from destruction. I was pleased at what I had done.

Then I remembered one of the most important laws of Lilliput. Urinating in the palace grounds was a crime punished by death! I was now worried, but the Emperor sent me a message. He said that he would order the court to pardon me for my crime. I learnt later that the Empress hated me for what I had done. She was very angry, and she decided never to return to the palace.

---

2. extinguish : put out the flames.

THINK!

Think about the questions below.

a What reasons does the Emperor have to be grateful to Gulliver?
b Why does the Emperor begin to distrust Gulliver?
c Do you like the Emperor less after you have read Chapter 3? Why?

The text and beyond • page 84
Values & Feelings • page 110

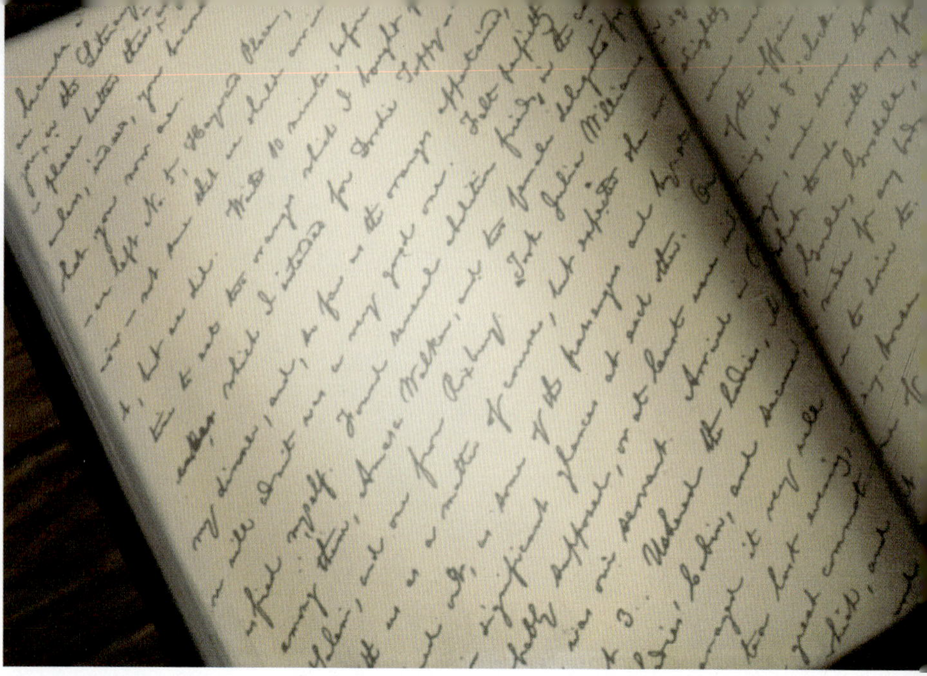

CHAPTER 4

Goodbye, Lilliput

I want to tell the world about the kingdom of Lilliput. One day I will publish a book about the people's lives and their habits. It will be a very big book! However, I have time and space here to tell you only the most important things about this interesting country.

It is important to remember that the people of Lilliput are very small. They are about six inches tall, and all the animals and trees are in proportion. The tallest horse is about five inches high, and a sheep about one inch. Some of the animals are so small that I could not see them easily. Birds, for example, are about the same size as flies in England. The tallest trees in Lilliput are seven feet high.

Goodbye, Lilliput

The Lilliputians are very educated people, but their way of writing is strange. They do not write from left to right like the Europeans, or from right to left like the Arabs. They do not write from the top of the page downwards, like the Chinese, or from the bottom upwards. They write from one corner of the paper to the opposite corner!

The laws of Lilliput are also very different to English laws. They regard trade as very important, and they think that trade depends on honesty. So they always punish fraud[1] with death. I remember once I asked the Emperor to save a prisoner who had been found guilty of fraud.

'Death is too serious a punishment,' I said. 'This man's crime is only that he told lies to his friend, and robbed him.'

The Emperor was very angry with me. He explained that this kind of robbery is the worst crime in the world.

Another strange thing about Lilliput is this. They punish bad behaviour, as we do in England. But they also reward good behaviour, which we never do in England. A Lilliputian who has obeyed all the laws of the country for a long time, is given a special title and some money by the government.

Their ideas about children are very different to ours. They do not believe that parents should choose their children's education. All children are taken away from their parents when they are young, and are sent to nursery schools. When they are older, children go to different schools. The choice of school depends on the family the children come from.

The children from important families go to schools where they learn about religion, honour, justice, and courage. Their professors are always with them, and the children are not allowed to talk to the servants in the school. Their parents can visit them once or twice a year, but they cannot bring them presents.

---

1. fraud : taking money by telling lies.

CHAPTER 4

Girls also go to schools, where they learn the same things as boys. They are also taught about family life. Girls are not allowed to talk to the servants in their schools. The result of this is that they do not hear the silly stories of ignorant women. In general, the women of Lilliput are sensible and intelligent.

The children of ordinary people go to schools where they learn various trades and professions.

The children of the poorest people do not go to school, because they do not have to learn anything to do their work. Poor people in Lilliput are given a government pension when they are old or ill, and there are no beggars[2] in the country.

I lived in Lilliput for nearly a year, and this is what my daily life was like. I made myself a table and chair from one of the biggest trees I could find. Two hundred women worked to make clothes for me. They used different techniques for measuring me, and these techniques amused me. The first method was to determine the length of my clothes. I lay on the ground, and one woman stood near my head, and another stood near my leg. They had a long piece of rope which they used as a measure of my height. When they wanted to make a jacket for me, they asked me to kneel[3] on the ground. Then they placed a ladder against my neck. A man climbed to the top of the ladder, and threw a length of rope down to the ground. This showed them the correct length of the jacket they wanted to make.

Three hundred cooks worked to prepare my food every day. I lifted twenty waiters onto my table. They threw ropes over the side of the table to the ground below. The cooks attached the barrels of wine and plates of food to the ropes, and the waiters pulled the food up to the table.

---

2. **beggar**: person who asks for money in the street.
3. **kneel**: go down on your knees.

CHAPTER 4

One night a very important Lilliputian came to see me at the temple. His visit there was a secret, he said.

'You are in danger,' he told me. 'The Emperor does not like you, and he wants to punish you.'

'Punish me!' I said. I was very surprised. 'Why does the Emperor want to punish me? I helped him to defeat the Blefuscu navy! And I saved the palace from the fire.'

'That's true,' the man agreed. 'But then you made a mistake. The Emperor wanted to destroy Blefuscu completely, and you refused to help him.'

'War is a terrible thing,' I replied. 'I didn't want to kill lots of people.'

'You're right,' the man admitted. 'But now the Emperor thinks you are his enemy. And then he was offended at the way you saved the palace – he says it was an insult to Lilliput!'

Then the important man told me what the Emperor and his ministers were planning.

'Some of his government ministers want to kill you,' he explained. 'But the Emperor has decided not to kill you. He thinks it will be

Goodbye, Lilliput

enough to remove your eyes. He wants to blind [4] you, Gulliver!'

I was horrified. I had thought the Emperor was my friend. I had helped his country in the war against Blefuscu – and now he wanted to take away my eyes! I decided to leave Lilliput immediately.

I travelled to Blefuscu, where the Emperor was very kind to me.

One day I went for a walk on the beach. I was feeling sad and unhappy, and I was thinking about England. Suddenly I saw a boat in the water. It was a real ship's boat, not one of the little boats of the Blefuscu people. This was a real boat, big enough for someone of my size! I was very excited, and I ran into the sea. I swam out to the boat, and climbed into it. Then I took the boat back to the shore, and tied it up carefully.

I told the Emperor of Blefuscu about the boat.

'I'm lonely here,' I told him. 'I want to go back to England. Maybe I can use that boat to go home, if you will help me. It'll be a long journey, but I'm sure I can do it.'

'Very well,' he said, 'I'll help you. I'll give you food and drink to put in the boat.'

---

4. blind : take away the ability to see.

CHAPTER 4

The Emperor ordered his men to prepare my boat. They gave me a large quantity of meat and wine. They also put some animals into the boat – six cows and two bulls, and six ewes [5] and two rams. [6] After a few days everything was ready.

I sailed away from Blefuscu. The sea was very big and lonely. After some days, I saw a large ship, and I followed it. It was an English ship, and one of the sailors saw me. They stopped, and took me on board. They were going to England, and they took me with them.

The captain of the ship was a friendly man. I told him about my adventures in Lilliput and Blefuscu. He did not believe me.

'Little men!' he laughed. 'You tell a good story, sir,' he said, 'but it's an impossible story, all the same.' And he laughed again.

'Then where do you think this came from?' I asked him. I put my hand in my pocket, and took out one of the tiny sheep from Blefuscu. I showed it to the captain. Now he believed my story!

---

5. **ewe** : female sheep.
6. **ram** : male sheep.

THINK!

Answer these questions 'yes' or 'no' and say why. Would you like to be:

1. a school child in Lilliput? 2. a female Lilliputian? 3. a poor person? 4. the child of a poor family? 5. an old person who is poor? 6. the Emperor? 7. a businessperson in Lilliput? 8. a citizen of Blefuscu? 9. Gulliver in Lilliput?

> **The text and beyond** • page 86
> **Values & Feelings** • page 110

CHAPTER 5

The Land of the Giants

My next voyage was on the ship *Adventure*. I often thought about my experiences in Lilliput and Blefuscu. I hoped that the two countries were at peace. Even though it was good to be back in England, I wanted to go travelling again.

However, the journey on the *Adventure* did not begin well.

There was a very big storm and a terrible wind. The wind blew the ship off course,¹ and we did not know where we were. Then one of the sailors saw that we were near land. We needed some fresh

---

1. **off course :** away from the intended direction.

CHAPTER 5

water, so some of us decided to take a ship's boat to the land.

When we came to the beach, we could not see any houses. I walked a little distance, but there was no sign of a village or town.

'No one lives here,' I thought. I was disappointed, and I turned to walk back to the boat. Then I saw that the other sailors were already in our boat. They were going away from the land very fast – and there was a huge creature following them in the water! The sailors were very frightened. I watched as they took the boat back to the ship.

Now I was alone, and I was frightened. I was afraid of the huge creature. I ran away from the beach. I ran to the top of a hill, and then I had a surprise. There were fields here – but they were not ordinary fields of corn and grass. Everything was very big. Then I saw a man – but he was as tall as a church! The corn was much taller than me, and I hid in it.

The giant called some other people. They were all giants, too. They began to cut the corn where I was hiding. I was very scared, and I cried out loudly. The first giant heard my cry, and he stopped work. He looked at the corn, and then he looked at the ground. He saw me. He reached down and picked me up. He held me between his fingers and looked at me for a while. I was very frightened to be so high in the air. I thought he would throw me onto the ground. I spoke to him, to show that I was a man like him. He seemed pleased that I could speak. Then I used signs to explain that his fingers were

CHAPTER 5

hurting my sides. He understood what I wanted to say, and he put me gently in his pocket. He carried me to the farmer.

'Look at this,' he said.

He put his hand in his pocket, and took me out. 'What do you think it is?' he asked.

The farmer looked at me for a moment.

He put me on the ground, and studied me carefully for a moment. He looked at my clothes, which he seemed to think were a natural part of my body.

'It's an animal,' he said. 'But I don't know what kind of animal it is.'

'I'm not an animal!' I shouted. 'I'm a man, like you.'

I walked backwards and forwards in front of the farmer and his men. I wanted to show them that I would not run away. They sat on the ground around me, and watched me with interest. I took off my hat. Then I pulled out my money and gave it to him. He looked at the money for a while, but he did not know what it was. Then I tried to speak to him.

'It can speak!' the farmer said. 'I don't know what it is – but I think I'll keep it.'

The farmer took me to his house. Everybody was eating dinner when we arrived. The farmer asked his wife what she thought of me. At first she thought I was a horrible little insect. She was frightened of me, the way English ladies are frightened of spiders. Then, when she saw that I understood what was happening, she lost her fear. She soon became a good friend.

The farmer put me on the table, and he gave me something to eat and drink. The farmer's son, who was about ten years old, then reached forward and picked me up. He held me in the air by my legs, and I was very frightened. The farmer was angry with his son, and ordered him to put me down. Then he slapped[2] his son on the

---

2. **slap** : hit with the hand.

The Land of the Giants

ear very hard, and told him to leave the table. I remembered how children can be cruel to little animals, and I decided to make a friend of the boy. I used signs to show the farmer that I wanted him to forgive his son. The farmer smiled, and told his son to return to the table. When he had sat down again, I went to the boy and kissed his hand.

The family cat came into the room during dinner. I was very scared of this huge animal, but I was determined not to show my fear. I walked up and down in front of the animal for a while, and the enormous cat seemed frightened of me! Then the nurse [3] brought in the baby of the family, who was about one year old. The baby saw me, and wanted to play with me. It put me into its mouth, and I thought it would eat me. I cried out very loudly, and the baby dropped me. Luckily, her mother caught me, or I would have been killed in the fall.

After dinner the farmer's wife put me onto her bed to sleep. She covered me with a handkerchief, and I soon fell asleep.

---

3. **nurse :** someone who looks after children.

CHAPTER 5

I was woken by a strange noise on the bed. I looked up, and there were two enormous rats on the bed – they were as big as dogs! I took out my sword, and attacked them. I killed one of the rats, and the second one ran away. Now I knew that it was dangerous to be small!

When the farmer's wife came into the room, she saw the body of the rat on the bed. She was very happy that I was not hurt.

The farmer and his wife had a daughter. She was nine years old, and she became my friend. She looked after me very well, and she taught me many things. She told me that the name of the country was Brobdingnag. She gave me lessons in their language. I called her Glumdalclitch, which is the word for 'little nurse' in their language. She called me Grildrig, which means 'little man' in their language.

THINK!

Imagine that you are in the Land of the Giants. How do you feel? Choose four items from the list. Explain why you chose them.

> afraid   amazed   bored   confident   disgusted
> in danger   sad   worried

Which of these qualities do you need? Choose four. Explain your choice.

> bravery   caution   fear   honesty   intelligence
> inventiveness   kindness   love

The text and beyond • page 88
Values & Feelings • page 110

CHAPTER 6

Entertaining the Giants

I enjoyed living with the farmer and his family. Time passed quickly. Many visitors came to the house because they had heard about the little man that the farmer had found in his field. The news spread fast through the village. I was famous in the area.

Everybody in the village wanted to see me and this gave one of the farmer's friends an idea.

'You could make a lot of money,' he told the farmer. 'Everybody in the village has seen the little man. Why don't you take him into town on market day? Make the people pay you to see him.'

The farmer thought this was a good idea. Glumdalclitch did not like the idea, because she was afraid the people would hurt me.

Entertaining the Giants

She also knew that I was very modest, and that I would not want to perform for the public.

The next morning, however, the farmer took Glumdalclitch and me to town. They put me into a box on one of the horses, and the journey was very uncomfortable for me. The horse moved very violently, and it was like being in a ship during a storm.

When we arrived at the town, we stayed in a hotel. The farmer told the people in the town about me, and lots of them came to see me. We organised a show for them.

'Stand up!' Glumdalclitch told me.

I stood up, and bowed[1] politely to the people in the room. They laughed, and clapped their hands.

'Take out your sword!' she said next.

I took out my sword, and looked fiercely at the people in the room. Once again, everybody laughed and clapped their hands.

The farmer made a lot of money, and he decided to travel to other towns. We went from town to town. Everyone came to see us, and I was very popular.

---

1. bow : lower the top part of the head and body as a polite gesture.

CHAPTER 6

We lived like this for a long time. It was a terrible life for me. I did not like to be a spectacle for the people. I was unhappy, and I became ill. Every day I lost strength, and I thought I was going to die. Glumdalclitch was worried about me, but her father just wanted to make as much money as possible from me. He did not care about me at all.

One day we came to the capital city of Brobdingnag. We performed our show for the people as usual. A lot of people came to see me, and the farmer was happy. We decided to stay in the city for a while.

Soon the whole city was talking about me. One day a man from the palace came to talk to the farmer.

'The Queen wants to see this little man,' he said. 'Bring him to the palace tonight.'

The farmer, Glumdalclitch and I were very excited. We decided to perform a very special show for the Queen. We wanted to please her.

THINK!

Gulliver doesn't like performing for spectators, but musicians, dancers, singers and actors enjoy performing in public. Choose three items from the box to describe Gulliver's probable feelings and the feelings of an experienced professional performer.

confident   embarrassed   proud   shy   miserable

Gulliver probably felt: ....
....

Performers feel: ....
....

> **The text and beyond** • page 90
> **Values & Feelings** • page 110

CHAPTER 7

A Dangerous Life

My life changed after the special show for the Queen. It was a great success. She was the perfect audience. I bowed to her and she smiled; I took out my sword and she pretended to be frightened. At the end of the show, she clapped very loudly.

'What a wonderful little man!' she said to the farmer. 'I want to keep him. Will you sell him to me?'

'Yes, I'll sell him to you, Your Majesty,' the farmer told her.

I was sad, because I liked Glumdalclitch. Then I had a good idea. I approached the Queen. I could speak a few words of their language now, and I asked her to do something for me.

The Queen smiled at me.

'What is it, little man?' she asked. 'What can I do for you?'

'Can Glumdalclitch stay here with me, Your majesty?' I asked.

'Of course she can!' the Queen said. 'You two are friends, aren't you?'

CHAPTER 7

That is how my life with the Queen of Brobdingnag began.

The Queen introduced me to the King, and he and I became friends very quickly. The King asked me a lot of questions about England. He was very surprised that everybody in England was small like me.

The King and Queen ordered a special box for me. It was made of wood, and there was a table inside, and some small chairs and a bed. The inside of the box was covered with soft material, so that I would not be hurt when someone carried it from one place to another. I kept a collection of interesting objects in the box. One of these was a servant's tooth – it was more than a metre in length!

It was a happy time for me, but there were many dangers because of my small size. There are some incidents [1] that I remember particularly.

Every morning Glumdalclitch carried my box to the window.

---

1. **incident**: event.

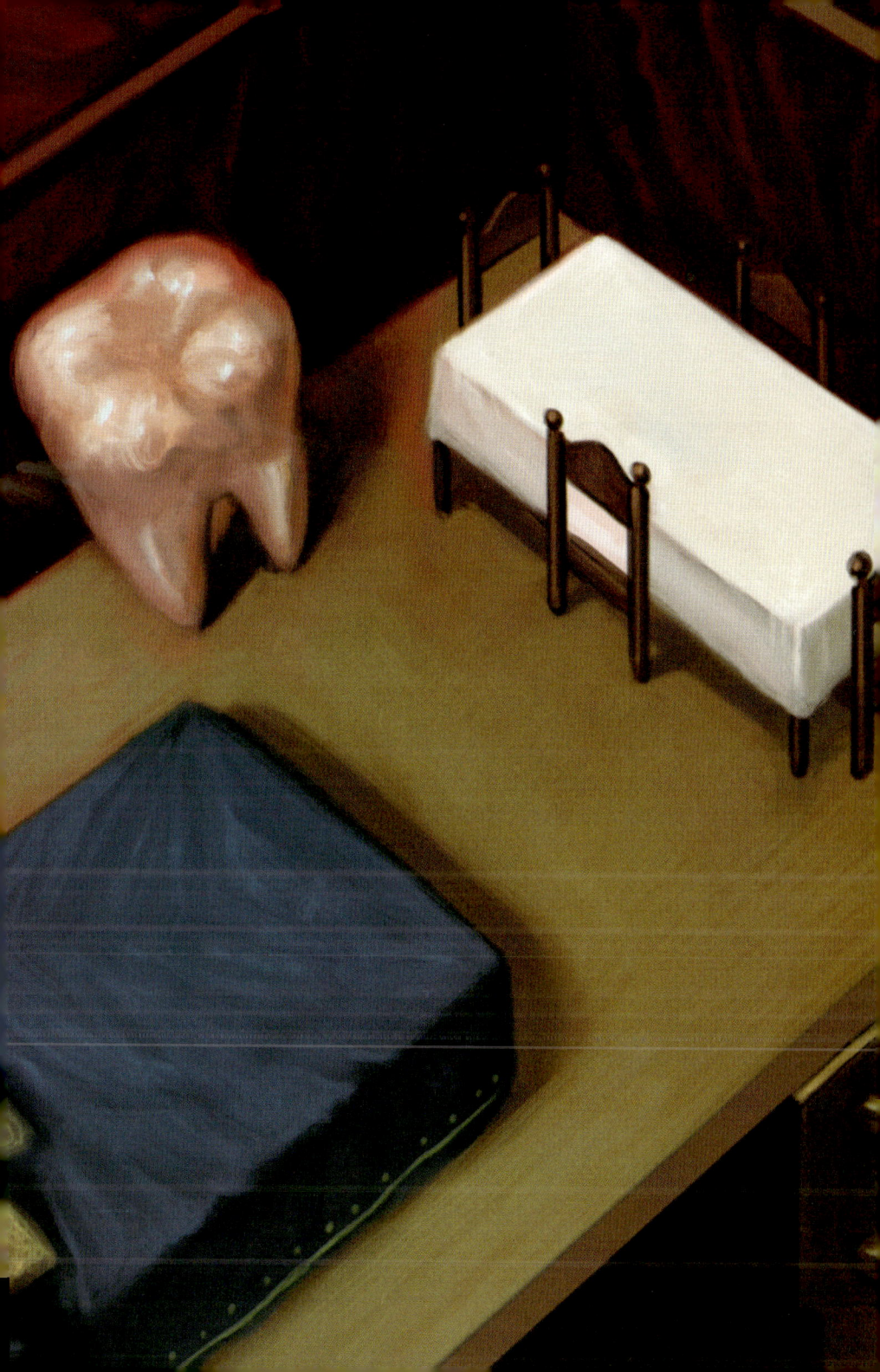

CHAPTER 7

One day she carried me to the window as usual, and then she left me there. Some huge wasps [2] came in through the window, and entered the box. They were the size of birds in England, and they were very fierce. I was frightened of them. I took out my sword and fought them. I killed four of them. Luckily, the others flew away.

Another dangerous occasion that I remember was this. Glumdalclitch left me in the garden one day, and the weather was very bad. First it rained, and then it hailed [3] very hard. The hailstones were the size of tennis-balls, and they hurt me badly. I managed to hide under a tree, but I was still hit by some of them.

Another danger came from an idea that the Queen had. She knew that I liked boats, and she ordered one of her servants to make a little boat for me. The servant put the boat into a tank of water on the table. I spent many hours in this boat. One day, however, a frog jumped out of the water into the boat. I thought the boat would sink, and I was frightened. I was lucky, and I managed to push the frog out of the boat.

The King and I had many conversations. He was a friendly man, but he did not understand anything about science. He was very surprised when I told him about the English army. He could not understand when I described the cannons that the army uses. When I offered to build a cannon for his own army, he became angry.

'No, Gulliver, I forbid it!' he said. 'I don't understand what these cannons are, but they seem terrible things. Never mention this subject again, please!'

My real problems in Brobdingnag started with the Queen's dwarf. [4] Before my arrival at the palace, he had been the smallest

---

2. wasp :

3. hail : when frozen rain falls from the sky.
4. dwarf : very small person.

person anyone had ever seen. I was much, much smaller than him, and he was jealous. He played all sorts of tricks on me – some of them were very dangerous.

We were having dinner with the Queen one night. The dwarf suddenly picked me up, and dropped me into a bowl of cream. The bowl was very deep, and I nearly drowned. Luckily Glumdalclitch was there, and she saved me. Another evening the dwarf attacked me again at dinner. This time he picked me up and pushed me into a bone on the Queen's plate. He attacked me a third time in the garden one afternoon. I was walking under some apple trees. He climbed into one of the trees, and shook the branches. [5] The apples, which were the size of barrels, fell onto the ground near me. It was a very dangerous and foolish thing to do.

---

5. **branch**: part of a tree which grows from the trunk.

CHAPTER 7

It was not only the dwarf who was dangerous. Animals were also a danger to me, because I was so small. One day the gardener's dog picked me up in his mouth. I was very frightened, and I thought he was going to eat me. The dog carried me very gently to the gardener, and dropped me at his feet. But the worst fright I had was with a monkey. The monkey came into a room of the palace. He picked me up, and carried me away. He seemed to think I was a baby monkey. He tried to give me food to eat, and then he climbed onto the roof of the palace with me in his hand. I was terrified. Some of the Queen's servants saw what happened. They ran to get ladders, and they climbed onto the roof to save me.

I spent about two years in Brobdingnag. Once again I began to think of home, and to be lonely. I was tired of being special because of my size. I wanted to go back to England.

One day the King decided to visit one of his palaces near the sea. He wanted me and Glumdalclitch to go with him, as usual. We travelled to the palace together. When we arrived, Glumdalclitch did not feel very well, and she went to bed.

One of the King's servants carried my box to the beach. I was inside, and I enjoyed looking at the waves from the window. The servant put the box down, and then he went back inside the palace. It was a hot day, and I fell asleep in the box.

I woke up suddenly when the box began to move. I looked out of the window, and the ground was a long way away – I was up in the air! I couldn't understand what had happened. Then I looked again, and I saw that a huge eagle⁶ was flying with the box in its mouth. I was very frightened, and I did not know what to do.

Then I heard another noise. I looked out of the window, and there were two large birds flying towards the eagle. They attacked the

6. eagle :

A Dangerous Life

eagle. They had a terrible fight. In the middle of the fight the eagle dropped the box.

The box fell into the sea with a great crash. I thought the box would break, but it was very strong. It floated in the water for a long time.

The captain of an English ship saw the box in the water. He ordered his men to bring it onto the ship. The sailors were very surprised when they saw a man inside it.

The captain asked me to tell him my story, and I did. He did not believe the things I told him about Brobdingnag.

'Giants!' he said. 'You don't expect me to believe that, do you? Giants don't really exist, my friend!'

'Then where do you think this came from?' I asked him. I went into the box for a moment, and took out the servant's tooth that I kept there. I showed it to the captain. Now he believed my story!

THINK!

Choose items from the box to answer the questions about the court dwarf below.

> anger   contentment   disappointment   jealousy   pride   shock

a What feelings did the court dwarf probably experience

before Gulliver arrived? .... & ....
when he first saw Gulliver? .... & ....
when his attacks failed? .... & ....

b How do you feel about the dwarf's behaviour? Choose a, b or c.

  a He was wrong but I understand his feelings.
  b I hate him because he tried to kill Gulliver.
  c I think he was right because Gulliver didn't belong there.

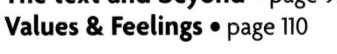
The text and beyond • page 92
Values & Feelings • page 110

CHAPTER 8

The Flying Island

I soon began another voyage. My friend Captain Robinson came to see me. He wanted to sail to the East Indies in his ship the *Hope-Well*. I did not want to travel again so soon because I had been back in England for only about ten days. However, he promised to pay me a lot of money to go with him. In the end I agreed.

There was bad news when the *Hope-Well* arrived in the East Indies. The goods which Captain Robinson wanted to buy were not ready.

'I'll have to stay here and wait,' Captain Robinson told me. 'But you don't have stay here with me, Gulliver. Let's buy a smaller ship, and you can go to the islands near here and buy and sell goods.'

The Flying Island

I agreed, and soon I was in command of a little ship of my own. Unfortunately this little ship was attacked by pirates. They came on board, and they stole everything, including the ship itself. They were very fierce, and I thought they were going to kill me. They changed their minds,[1] though, and decided to put me into a canoe with enough food and water for four days.

I knew there were some islands in this part of the sea. I spent a few days going from one island to another. The islands were all small ones, and there were no people on them. There was also very little food. I began to think that I would die on one of these islands, and I was very unhappy.

One day I saw something very strange in the sky. It was afternoon, and the sun was very hot. Suddenly the sky became dark, and I could not see the sun at all. I looked up, and saw a huge object in the sky. It seemed to be an island, and it was flying! I looked at it through my telescope, and I saw people on the island. I was very surprised to see a flying island with people on it, and I did not know what to do.

I decided to call out to the people. Perhaps they would help me to escape. I shouted very loudly, and waved my arms. Some of the people on the flying island heard me, and they looked down at me. Soon there was a crowd of people looking down at me.

The island began to come close to me. Someone threw down a piece of rope with a chair tied to it. I climbed into the chair, and I was pulled up towards the mysterious island.

A crowd of people was waiting to welcome me when I arrived. They told me that the name of their island was Laputa. They were strange people. Their heads were very flat, and one eye looked up to the sky and the other eye looked in the opposite direction. The clothes of the rich people were strange, too. They had pictures of stars

---

1. change their minds : have a new idea.

CHAPTER 8

and musical instruments on them. The rich people all had servants, and I saw that the servants carried sticks with them. Sometimes the servants touched their masters on the mouth or ears with the stick. I did not understand why they did this until someone explained it to me. The rich people of the island were all mathematicians and thinkers. They were very busy with their thoughts. When someone wanted to speak to them, they did not notice. Their servants had to touch them with a stick to make them listen.

Some of the people took me to the King's palace, and he invited me to have dinner with him. The King was a very polite man, and he wanted me to be his guest and learn their language.

The people of the island were only interested in mathematics and music. They spent their time solving mathematical problems, and thinking about music. They were very good at making theories, but they were not practical people at all. They could not make proper clothes or build decent houses.

No one wanted to talk to me about my adventures, or to learn about my country. All they wanted to do was talk about mathematics and music. After a while, they stopped talking to me completely.

There was a very important man at the court who became a friend of mine. He was a cousin of the King, and had a very important position in the country. Everyone thought he was stupid because he was not good at mathematics or music. He was the only man on the island who was interested in talking to me about my adventures and about England. He asked me many questions about the places I had visited, and their systems of government.

After a month on the flying island, I wanted to leave. The people were kind to me, but they only wanted to talk about mathematics and music. They were not interested in me.

I learnt that the King of the island was also the King of the country below the island. This country is called Balnibarbi, and its

capital city is called Lagado. I asked the King's permission to visit the other parts of his kingdom, and he gave it to me. My friend, the King's cousin, was sorry to see me go.

'I'll miss you,' he said, 'I've enjoyed our conversations. But when you are in Balnibarbi, please see my friend Lord Munodi. He'll show you the country.'

I met Lord Munodi in the capital city, Lagado. He was a very polite and intelligent man, and he took me on a tour of the country. I saw that the whole country was very badly organised. The houses in the towns were very ugly, and the people seemed poor. The land in the countryside seemed rich, but there were very few farms. I told Lord Munodi what I thought.

'Every country has its own traditions,' he said quietly. 'Our country is certainly different to England.'

He took me to see his own farm, and this was very different to the other farms in the country. Everything was very well organised, and the people seemed happy and rich.

'What a difference!' I said. 'Your farm is the best in the whole country.'

'Thank you,' he replied. 'I'm happy that you like my farm.'

Then he looked very sad.

'But it will not always be like this. I have just received some bad news. I will soon have to change everything, and make this farm like the others you have seen.'

I was very surprised at what he told me, and I asked him to explain. Then he told me about the recent history of Balnibarbi.

'About forty years ago,' he said, 'the country was all like this. The towns were well organised, and the farms were rich. Then some people from Balnibarbi went up to Laputa. They stayed there for about five months. When they came back here, they brought with them ideas about mathematics and music. They asked the King to begin an Academy at Lagado. That is the cause of the problem. The professors at the Academy have all got new ideas – but none of their ideas work. They are destroying the country.'

I told Lord Munodi that I wanted to see this Academy, and he asked a friend to take me there. The Academy was one of the strangest places I have ever seen.

It was full of professors, and each professor was working on a different project.

CHAPTER 8

The first professor that I saw had a special project. He wanted to extract the sunlight from cucumbers. [2]

'We can use the sunlight to heat the houses in winter,' he told me. He was sure that his project would be a great success.

There was a school of languages in the academy, and I went there to see what the professors were doing. One professor had a project to make conversations shorter. He was working on a language that only had nouns in it.

Another professor had a project for a new kind of language.

'Words are really the names of things,' he explained to me. 'In my new language, we use things instead of words. Everybody carries a bag with the things in it that he wants to talk about. When he wants to talk, he brings out the thing he wants to talk about, and shows it to the people.'

---

2. cucumber :

THINK!

What is Swift laughing at in this Chapter? Choose the two best answers from a-e.

a Scientists in general?
b Mathematicians and musicians?
c People who create theories that are useless in real life?
d Farmers who try to improve their farms?
e Professors who do not understand life in the real world?

> **The text and beyond** • page 94
> **Values & Feelings** • page 110

CHAPTER 9

The Land of Ghosts

Let me tell you about two more strange lands. One of them is the island of Luggnagg. First of all, I sailed to the port of Maldonado. Then I planned to go to Luggnagg and, after that, to reach Japan. I wanted to return to England and I knew that many ships sailed from Japan to Europe.

When I arrived at Maldonado, I learnt that the next ship for Luggnagg was expected in a month. I spent a few days in the port of Maldonado, and the local people were very kind to me. One of them offered to take me to the little island of Glubbdubrib.

'It will amuse you,' he said, 'and it isn't far. We can go there together, and when we come back, your ship for Luggnagg will be here.'

CHAPTER 9

I accepted his kind offer, because I was curious to see Glubbdubrib. I knew that the name of the island means 'magician'[1] in their language, and I wanted to see what an island of magicians was like!

When we arrived on the island, we went to the Governor's palace. The Governor welcomed us kindly, but there was something strange about his servants. They were not dressed in modern clothes, and they were very white and pale. The Governor asked us to sit down, and began to question me about my adventures. Then he clapped his hands, and the servants in the room suddenly disappeared. One minute they were there, and the next they were gone! I was very surprised, and a little frightened. Then the Governor told me the truth about his servants.

'They're not real people,' he said, 'they're ghosts. I'm a magician, and I can make dead people appear and disappear.'

He clapped his hands again, and the servants reappeared instantly.

We stayed about ten days on the island, and we saw the Governor of the island every day. I became used to the strange servants, and I was interested in the governor's magic. He told me that he could use his power to make any dead person appear. He asked me if I would like to meet any famous people from history. He offered to make them appear for me.

'You can ask them any questions you like,' he told me. 'They are ghosts, and they will tell you the truth.'

I asked to see some of the heroes of the past. First I saw Alexander the Great, and the great General Hannibal. Then I saw Pompey the Great, Caesar and Brutus. Next I asked to see famous poets and thinkers from the past, and I saw Homer and Aristotle. I also saw some of the heroes of modern times.

I asked them many questions about famous events in history, but their answers made me sad. I learnt that many of these heroes had

---

1. **magician** : someone who makes magic.

CHAPTER 9

not been brave at all during their lives. They had been dishonest, and they had been cruel. I was very disappointed in my heroes.

We stayed about ten days on the island of Glubbdubrib before returning to Maldonado. I then took a ship for the island of Luggnagg.

The King of Luggnagg welcomed me kindly, and I spent some time at the palace. I made friends with some of the most important men on the island, and we had many long conversations.

One day, one of my friends asked me if I knew about the Struldbruggs.

'No,' I replied, 'I've never heard of the Struldbruggs. Who are they?'

'The Struldbruggs,' he explained, 'are people who do not die. They live for ever.'

'How wonderful!' I cried. I was very excited. 'I'm sure the Struldbruggs are very wise. Do they share their wisdom with the people? Do they help and advise the King? Think how happy they are, these men who never die!'

My friend smiled.

'You think they are happy, these men who never die?' he asked me. 'You think they are wise, and good, and happy, don't you?'

'Certainly,' I replied. 'I'm sure they are wise, and good, and happy.'

'Listen to me,' my friend said, 'and I'll tell you the truth about the Struldbruggs. They are born with a special mark on their heads,' he began. 'Everyone knows who they are. They behave like ordinary people until they are about thirty years old. Then they become sad, and they are sad until they are about eighty years old. When

The Land of Ghosts

they are eighty years old, they are like other old men. They forget things, and they become ill. After the age of eighty, they lose all their friends, and they never make new friends. Their sufferings are terrible,' my friend said.

'When they are ninety years old, they have no memory at all,' he continued. 'They cannot remember the names of their children. They cannot read, because they cannot remember the words of a sentence. After two hundred years, they cannot even speak to people. This is because the language of the country changes, and they cannot learn the new words.'

This story of the Struldbruggs made me very sad. I left Luggnagg shortly afterwards. I travelled to Japan, where I found a ship for England.

THINK!

Some of the 'heroes' in our history or our mythology did these things. Which things from a-f might Gulliver see as cruel/stupid and which as good?

a They started wars. (e.g. Napoleon)
b They killed people. (Henry VIII)
c They helped the poor. (Robin Hood)
d They killed themselves (Cleopatra)
e They made big mistakes. (Adam and Eve)
f They fell in love. (Romeo and Juliet)

Think of a historical 'hero'. What are the good and bad things which he/she did?

The text and beyond • page 96
Values & Feelings • page 110

CHAPTER 10

The Land of Wise Horses

Pirates stole my ship! This is how it happened. I had been very happy after I returned to my home in England. I decided not to go on any more voyages. But someone offered me a ship of my own, the *Adventure*, and I began another journey.

This voyage was very unlucky.

Many of the crew of the *Adventure* became ill on the journey, and some of them died. Soon there were not enough sailors to drive the ship. I decided to stop in Barbados to find more sailors. This was a mistake, however, because many of the new sailors were really pirates.

The new sailors waited until the ship was at sea, and then they attacked me, and one of them took command of the ship. They stopped the ship when they saw land, and they left me there. No one knew the name of the country. Once again, I was alone in a foreign land.

I did not know if there were people in this country, but I decided to look for a village or town. I walked for a long time, but I did not see any buildings, or any farms. At last I saw several animals in a field. These animals were very ugly, and looked a little like monkeys. I watched them for a while, and then continued my walk.

While I was walking, one of these animals came up to me. It raised one of its hands, and tried to touch me on the face. I took out my sword, and hit the animal to drive it away.¹ The animal cried out angrily, and about forty of the horrible creatures appeared. They surrounded me, and began shouting and making a noise. I was frightened, and I hoped someone would come to rescue me.

Suddenly all the animals ran away. This surprised me, because I did not see anyone. There was only a horse walking quietly by itself. The horse came close to me, and looked at me for a long time. It walked around me, and it seemed very interested in me.

Soon another horse appeared, and a very strange thing happened. The two horses looked at each other, and both of them made the same noise. They seemed to talk to each other!

---

1. **drive it away :** make it go away.

CHAPTER 10

'This is a wonderful country,' I thought. 'The horses talk to each other! I want to see the people, to find out if they are as wonderful as the horses.'

At that moment the horses came very close to me, and touched my hands and face. They were very gentle, and they did not hurt me. Then they made a low noise, and I understood that they wanted me to follow them.

The horses and I walked for about three miles, until we arrived at a large building. I was happy to see a building.

'The people here will help me,' I thought, 'once they know I want to go back to England.'

We entered the building, and I was very surprised that there were no people in it. It was full of horses. Some of them were sitting down, which I thought was very strange. Others were working to prepare food. Then they took me into another room of the building. There was another horse in this room, and he seemed very important. The other horses behaved with great respect to the master horse. When he saw me, he said something. I heard the word Yahoo. The other horses repeated this word with anger and contempt.[2]

Then we all went to another building, and I saw some of the horrible animals which had attacked me. They were very dirty, and they were tied with ropes. The master horse looked at this creature, and then looked at me. All the horses were silent for a moment, and the master horse said the word Yahoo again. I looked at the ugly animals, and suddenly I was horrified. They were dirty, and they were covered in hair, but they were people!

Now we went back to the first building. The master horse was very surprised when I tried to use some of the words of their language. He tried to teach me more words, and he was very pleased that I could repeat them.

---

2. **contempt :** derision, disgust.

CHAPTER 10

I am good at learning languages, and after ten weeks I was able to understand the horses when they spoke to me. I learnt that they called themselves Houyhnhnm, which means horse. The master horse told me that they called the ugly creatures Yahoos.

'We thought you were a Yahoo as well,' he told me. 'You look the same, but you are intelligent and clean. When you spoke to us, we didn't know what to think. Yahoos can never learn to speak our language.'

I told him that I came from a different country. Then I told him about some of my adventures. When I told him about the ship, he looked unhappy.

'It's impossible,' he said. 'There isn't a country over the sea. And I don't understand this story of a ship. I don't know what a ship is, but

The Land of Wise Horses

it's impossible for creatures like you to make one. A Houyhnhnm couldn't make one – how could you?'

'In my country,' I explained to him, 'everything is different. The animals you call Yahoos are intelligent, like me. Horses in my country are not intelligent.'

'I don't believe you,' he replied. 'It's impossible to imagine a country where Yahoos are intelligent – and I cannot imagine a country where Houyhnhnms are not intelligent. You are inventing this story.'

Then I told the master horse about life in England. I explained that we use horses to pull carriages, and that we ride upon their backs. Again, he did not seem to think this was possible.

'Horses do not allow Yahoos to ride upon their backs,' he told me. 'What you say is impossible.'

I told him about the history of England and our famous wars with our enemies.

'This thing called war,' he said, 'is difficult for me to understand. You seem intelligent creatures, but you kill each other. It is a good thing you are not strong like horses – you cannot bite each other, or hurt each other very badly.'

'You are wrong,' I told him. 'It is true that our bodies are not strong, but we have very powerful weapons. We have bombs, guns, pistols, and swords. Many people are killed during our wars.'

Now the master horse was angry. He looked at me very seriously.

'Then your people are worse than the Yahoos we have here,' he said. 'The

CHAPTER 10

Yahoos here are stupid and horrible, it's true. But your people are intelligent, and there is no excuse for them.'

One day the master horse called me to him.

'I have been thinking about your people,' he said. 'I think I understand you now. It is true that you are intelligent, and the Yahoos here are not intelligent. They are stupid and wicked. But your people are intelligent and wicked – that's the difference between you and the Yahoos!'

During my stay with the Houyhnhnms I began to understand and admire them. They live very simple lives, and they love friendship and truth. They never fight with each other, and they never argue. They believe they can use their intelligence to solve all problems.

I began to understand the Houyhnhnms, and I began to hate human beings. The Houyhnhnms were gentle and noble, and human beings are violent and stupid. I knew that we were Yahoos. I was ashamed of being a Yahoo.

I listened to many conversations between the master horse and his friends. They spoke very wisely, and I grew to love them. I wanted to spend the rest of my life with the Houyhnhnms. But one day the master horse came to see me.

'I have something to tell you,' he said. 'The great Assembly of the Houyhnhnms has made a decision about you. They say that you are a Yahoo, and they want you to leave. I am sorry, but you must go back to your own country.'

This was very bad news for me. I did not want to return to England, and to the world of the Yahoos. I knew I must obey, however, and I built myself a little boat for the journey. All my Houyhnhnm friends came to say goodbye to me on the day I left their country.

I stopped my little boat at an island in the middle of the sea. There was a ship here from Portugal, and the sailors captured me.

The Land of Wise Horses

They took me to their captain, Don Pedro. He was very kind to me, and he said that I could travel to England with him.

'I don't want to come with you,' I said. 'I'm just a Yahoo – leave me alone.'

Don Pedro did not understand what I was talking about, and he asked me to explain. I told him the story of my adventure with the Houyhnhnms.

'They are very good, and they taught me a lot,' I said. 'Now I don't like people – we're all just stupid Yahoos!'

Don Pedro persuaded me to return to England and my family. At first I did not want to see my family or my children. I did not want to live with Yahoos.

I have now been back at home for five years, and I am still unhappy. I have had so many adventures, and I have learnt the truth about people. We are Yahoos. The knowledge makes me very sad. I miss my friends, the Houyhnhnms.

THINK!

Look at the list of qualities below.

a ambition **b** anger **c** cleanliness **d** dirtiness **e** friendship
f intelligence **g** love of peace **h** love of truth **i** love of war
j rational behaviour **k** respect **l** rudeness **m** simplicity
n stupidity **o** violence **p** wisdom

Which belong to the Houyhnhnms and which belong to the Yahoos? Which belong to people in Gulliver's own human society, in Swift's opinion?

Houyhnhnms	c, f,
Yahoos	b, d,
Human society	a, b,

> **The text and beyond** • page 98
> **Values & Feelings** • page 110

Popular travel books

The countries which Gulliver visits are not real ones, but Jonathan Swift describes the appearance of the people, their kind of government, and their habits and manners in realistic detail. Scholars believe that Swift used two famous collections of travel stories when writing *Gulliver's Travels*.
- Richard Hakluyt's *Principal Navigations*, *Voyages*, and *Discoveries of the English Nation*, published in 1600, describes some of the best-known voyages in English history. Hakluyt describes the voyage of Sir Francis Drake around the world, Sir Walter Raleigh's voyage to Venezuela, and John Davys's Arctic voyage.
- Samuel Purchas published his *Purchas His Pilgrims*, in 1625. This book has details of voyages to India, China, Japan and Africa, as well as a description of a voyage to Florida.

▶ **Robinson Crusoe** on his raft, escaping from the shipwreck (1719).

Sea voyages, and the discovery of new countries, were a very popular theme for 18th-century writers. In fact, Swift's contemporary, Daniel Defoe, wrote his very successful novel *Robinson Crusoe* in 1719. Defoe was also fascinated by the idea of sea voyages, adventure and exploration. Like Lemuel Gulliver, Robinson Crusoe's adventure begins when his ship sinks during a bad storm. Robinson is shipwrecked on a desert island where he must use his ingenuity[1] and intelligence in order to survive.

This was a great age of geographical discovery, and there were many expeditions exploring the seas and oceans of the world. There were stories of unknown continents in the Pacific Ocean, and of wonderful riches. Sailors brought back strange animals from their voyages, and some of them told fantastic tales about the places they had seen. The most famous discoverer of the century was Captain James Cook, who discovered Australia in 1770. His *An Account of a Voyage Round the World* was published in 1773.

1. **ingenuity :** ability to solve problems.

1 Look at the sentences below. Decide if each statement is correct or incorrect. If it is correct, mark A. If it is not correct, mark B.

                                                                                                 A B

1. The countries which Gulliver visits are real ones.
2. Jonathan Swift writes about the countries that Gulliver visits with a lot of detail.
3. Scholars think that Swift consulted books by Richard Hakluyt and Samuel Purchas when writing *Gulliver's Travels*.
4. Sir Walter Raleigh sailed around the world.
5. Sir Francis Drake sailed to the Arctic.
6. Sailors brought back treasure and riches from their voyages.
7. Captain Cook discovered New Zealand in 1770.

Now rewrite the incorrect sentences.

Gulliver's Travels on screen

Gulliver's Travels has been filmed many times for the cinema and TV. It has always been a challenge for the technology of the time to show Lilliputians and giants. The scene where Gulliver wakes up to find that he has been tied by the Lilliputians is always popular with audiences. Here are some of the film versions.

▶ **A scene** from the 1996 TV film.

A silent film

The earliest version is a French silent film from 1902. It was called in English *Gulliver's Travels Among the Lilliputians and the Giants*. The director, Georges Méliès, explored ways to make the people of Lilliput appear tiny next to Gulliver. In some scenes, he filmed the actors from a distance to make them seem smaller. In others, he combined different pieces of film to create the difference in size.

A Soviet 'Gulliver'

In 1935, a Russian film version of *Gulliver's Travels* was made, using 3,000 puppets. It was a very well-made and technologically clever film. The film was made during the time of the Soviet Union and Swift's story was changed to create a battle between capitalists and workers. A revolution by the workers of Lilliput against the Emperor was supported by Gulliver.

Focus on Lilliput

In 1939, an animated film was made in the USA inspired by the highly successful cartoons of Disney such as *Snow White*. Like many other films of *Gulliver's Travels*, it concentrated on his adventures in Lilliput. The film-makers added a love story between Prince David of Lilliput and Princess Glory of Blefuscu.

Cinema

In 1977, another film used a mixture of actors and animation. Gulliver, played by Richard Harris, a famous actor of that time, meets one of the giants from Brobdingnag but otherwise the story is limited to Lilliput and Blefuscu.

The complete 'Travels'

In 1996, the most magical, beautiful and complete film of Swift's original story was released as a TV mini-series. It featured many famous actors and used the latest technology of the 1990s.

This film told the story of all four voyages, not just Lilliput. CGI (computer generated imagery) was used to create special effects, such as giant wasps in Brobdingnag and the flying island of Laputa. The film is very faithful to Jonathan Swift's concept.

A 21st-century Gulliver

Jack Black stars as Gulliver in a 2010 film but the story has been changed a great deal. Gulliver is an American worker who goes to report on the Bermuda Triangle, a mysterious part of the Atlantic where ships and aeroplanes disappear. He finds himself in Lilliput and has many adventures which are not part of Swift's original story.

As you can see, *Gulliver's Travels* has been an inspiration for the film industry for more than a hundred years.

▶ **Gulliver** in the 1977 film.

Utopia and Dystopia

▶ **Sir Thomas More** by Hans Holbein the Younger, painted between 1497-1543.

Jonathan Swift was not the first writer to use an imaginary travel book as a way of discussing his ideas about society. Many writers have used an imaginary journey to explore political and philosophical ideas. Most writers describe a 'perfect' society which is based on the author's own political or philosophical ideas. Critics use the term 'utopian' to categorise this kind of book. Sometimes, however, the writer wants to criticise his own society by showing its defects, and the imaginary place is seen as being a terrible one. Critics use the term 'dystopian' for this kind of book.

Perhaps the most famous example of this kind of book is Sir Thomas More's *Utopia*, published in 1516. The book tells the story of how the author meets a traveller who has been to a wonderful country called Utopia ('Utopia' means 'no place'). The inhabitants of this land share their possessions, there is a national education system that benefits women as well as men, and religious freedom.

There are three 17th-century books which are connected with the idea of Utopia. Francis Bacon's *New Atlantis* (1627) tells the story of a visit to an imaginary island, Bensalem, while James Harrington's *The Commonwealth of Oceana* (1656) uses the imaginary country of Oceana to discuss the political problems of England after the Civil War and the execution of King Charles I. John Bunyan's *The Pilgrim's Progress*, published in 1684, is not really a 'utopian' or 'dystopian' fantasy, but it does include an imaginary journey. It is also one of the most famous books in the English language. It is based on a journey of the Christian hero from the City of Destruction to the Celestial City.

Two books – Edward Bellamy's *Looking Backward: 2000-1887* (published in 1888) and William Morris's *News from Nowhere* (1890) – both tell the story of a dream. The main characters both dream about a better society in the future where people are happy and free.

Samuel Butler's *Erewhon*, published in 1872, tells the story of the narrator's journey to the undiscovered country of Erewhon ('Nowhere'). The morality and social values of the country are described. The narrator learns that morality is associated with health and beauty, and crime with illness. Machinery is against the law. The country is governed by untrustworthy[1] philosophers. Erewhon is similar to *Gulliver's Travels* because it uses the imaginary journey to satirise contemporary society.

The two most famous dystopian novels of the 20th century are Aldous Huxley's *Brave New World*, published in 1932, and George Orwell's *Nineteen Eighty-Four*, published in 1949. *Brave New World* describes an imaginary world of the future where human life is based on a scientific control system. The book explores the loss of

---

1. **untrustworthy :** not to be trusted.

personal freedom in a perfectly controlled world. *Nineteen Eighty-Four* is also set in the future, and is also about the desire for personal freedom. Its hero, Winston Smith, tries to resist the police state, but is eventually defeated by the powers of Big Brother.

1 Write brief answers to the questions below.

1. Who are the three authors who wrote about 'utopias' before Swift?
2. In your opinion, is Lilliput a 'utopia'? Why/Why not?
3. Books from which century are about 'dystopia' rather than 'utopia'?
4. In Bellamy's and Morris's books the main characters, unlike Gulliver, do not go on a journey. How do they discover the imaginary lands?
5. Does the land of 'Erewhon' seem to be closer to a utopia or a dystopia? Give one reason for your answer.
6. In *Brave New World*, individual human beings are controlled by science. How are people controlled in *1984*?
7. Which three books have titles which in some way refer to the idea of 'nowhere'?

▶ **The writer** Aldous Huxley.

Activities

80 ► **The text and beyond**

Chapter 1	80
Chapter 2	82
Chapter 3	84
Chapter 4	86
Chapter 5	88
Chapter 6	90
Chapter 7	92
Chapter 8	94
Chapter 9	96
Chapter 10	98

100 **Extensive listening**

102 **Surf the net**

103 **Trinity** • Preparation

104 **Preliminary** • Preparation

107 **Exit test** • Let's revise the story

110 **Values & Feelings**

Chapter 1

THE TEXT AND BEYOND

1 Comprehension check • **Answer the questions below.**

1. What is Gulliver's profession? Why did he choose it?
2. What was the name of the ship?
3. Why did the sailors leave the ship?
4. Where did Gulliver fall asleep?
5. What happened to Gulliver while he was sleeping?
6. What did the men do when he tried to escape?
7. What did the men construct? Why?
8. Why did they use the temple as a place to imprison Gulliver?
9. Who were the first people who visited Gulliver in the temple?

2 Vocabulary • **Fill in the missing words from Chapter 1.**

> arrows   barrels   daring   escape   language
> prisoner   ropes   sheep   still   temple   tiny

When Gulliver woke up he saw **(1)** .... all around his body. There were hundreds of **(2)** .... men on the beach. They shot **(3)** .... at him when he tried to **(4)** .... He decided to lie very **(5)** ....

Gulliver did not understand their **(6)** .... so they spoke using signs. They told him that the name of this country was Lilliput and that he was the **(7)** .... of the Emperor.

Gulliver asked for food and they brought him cows, **(8)** .... and **(9)** .... of wine. They built a machine and many horses pulled Gulliver to the city. They took him to a **(10)** .... where he had many visitors including the Emperor himself. People arrived from all over the city to look at him and some very **(11)** .... people put ladders against his body and climbed up.

3 Vocabulary • Check the meaning of these words in your dictionary, then write them in the correct column below.

> anchor   captain   crew   deep
> rock   rope   sail   sailor   shallow   storm   wave

Sea	Ship

4 Style – A • Gulliver sometimes describes feelings and emotions. Look back at pages 11-12 and fill the gaps below with a single word.

1. I was .... I fell asleep on the ground.
2. I was very .... to see a tiny man.
3. The little men were ....
4. He told me not to be ....

B • But Gulliver often doesn't describe his own emotions. How do you think he felt when:

1. he realised the other sailors had drowned?
2. he woke and found that he couldn't move?
3. the arrows began to hit him?
4. they used chains and locks to tie him up again?
5. lots of people came to look at him?

Do you like this unemotional style? Does it make the story more convincing?

Chapter 2

THE TEXT AND BEYOND

1 Comprehension check • Answer the following questions.

1. What does the colonel do with the unfriendly soldiers?
2. What does Gulliver do with his penknife?
3. How long does it take Gulliver to learn the language of Lilliput?
4. Why does the Emperor want to search Gulliver?
5. What does Gulliver have to do before the Emperor gives him his freedom?
6. He watches two dances. What happens to the best dancer of the first dance?
7. What do they give the winner of the second dance?
8. Give one example of how Gulliver tries to please the Emperor.

2 Sequencing the story • Which of the two events a-j do NOT happen in Chapter 2? Write the other letters in the correct time sequence in the boxes below. The first is done for you.

a Gulliver sees some unusual dances.
b Gulliver learns the language of Lilliput.
c Gulliver shows that he is not cruel.
d Some frightened children hide in Gulliver's hair.
e Gulliver gets his freedom.
f Some soldiers attack Gulliver.
g Gulliver fires his gun.
h Gulliver punishes the soldiers who attack him.
i Gulliver is part of a military parade.
j The Emperor visits Gulliver a second time.
k The Lilliputians search Gulliver.

j								

3 Vocabulary • Match the pictures below with descriptions 1-6.

1. A very large piece of cloth
2. Some pieces of white material
3. Machine with pieces of metal on it
4. A very long tube of metal attached to a piece of wood
5. Machine that makes a big noise
6. Metal balls and some black powder

4 Writing descriptions • The Lilliputians describe the items they find in Gulliver's pockets. Here is a description of something in the modern world. What is it?

> Lots of large metal boxes with wheels. People climb inside and all the boxes move together. There are pieces of metal in the ground under the thing. It makes a lot of noise and moves quickly.

Imagine you are a Lilliputian and write descriptions of some of these: a computer, a football, a car, a bus, a mobile phone, a bicycle, a torch.

Chapter 3

THE TEXT AND BEYOND

1 Comprehension check • Put the sentences below into the correct order. The first has been done for you.

- a [1] A war starts between Blefuscu and Lilliput.
- b [   ] The Blefuscu sailors are frightened.
- c [   ] The Emperor says that Gulliver is a hero.
- d [   ] Gulliver tells the Emperor that he has a plan.
- e [   ] Gulliver walks into the sea.
- f [   ] Gulliver pulls the Blefuscu navy towards Lilliput.
- g [   ] Gulliver ties a piece of rope to each of the Blefuscu ships.

The past perfect

'In the past, the people of Lilliput and the people of Blefuscu *had agreed* about this.'
'One day, however, the Emperor's grandfather *had* an accident.'

We use the **past perfect** to show that one event in the past occurred before another one.

THE EARLIER PAST = before the main time of the story:	**THE PAST** = the main time of the story:
past perfect verbs are used: *they **had agreed**... they **had** both **believed**...*	**past simple** verbs are used: *he **had** an accident... he **ordered** the Lilliputians...*

We form the past perfect using **had** + **the past participle**

If there are two past actions, we often use the **past perfect** to emphasise which action happened earlier:

*Gulliver **had worked** in London before he **became** a ship's doctor.*

2 Grammar • Put the verbs in brackets into the past simple or the past perfect.

1. The crew jumped into the sea after the ship (*strike*) .... a rock.
2. The Lilliputians (*tie*) .... up Gulliver after he had fallen asleep.
3. When they (*finish*) .... making the machine, they put him on it.
4. I was the biggest man they (*see*) .... in their lives.
5. The Emperor (*give*) .... jobs to the men who had danced well.
6. Blefuscu (*be*) .... sure they would win until they saw Gulliver.
7. The arrows (*not hurt*) .... his eyes because he had put on his glasses.
8. The Empress was angry although Gulliver (*save*) .... the palace.

3 Ideas • Match the pieces of text from the story 1-6 with the general ideas a-f. The first has been done for you.

1. [d] They refused to obey the Emperor. There was a civil war.
2. [ ] Thousands of people had been killed in the war of the eggs.
3. [ ] They were sure they would be victorious.
4. [ ] He was very angry... Now he did not like me.
5. [ ] This act saved the palace from destruction.
6. [ ] The Empress hated me for what I had done.

a War is unpredictable.
b Powerful rulers are often ungrateful.
c Personal pride can stop you from acting fairly.
d Ridiculous things often cause wars.
e Wars are tragic.
f In some situations, impolite actions are necessary.

Chapter 4

THE TEXT AND BEYOND

1 Comprehension check • **Say if these sentences are true (T) or false (F). Correct the false ones.**

		T	F
1.	The people of Lilliput are about five inches tall.	☐	☐
2.	The tallest trees in Lilliput are about seven feet high.	☐	☐
3.	The Lilliputians write in the same way as we do.	☐	☐
4.	Only murder is always punished with death in Lilliput.	☐	☐
5.	People who always obey the law get a reward.	☐	☐
6.	Gulliver thinks that the girls' education is effective.	☐	☐
7.	The Emperor of Lilliput decides to punish Gulliver by killing him.	☐	☐
8.	Gulliver is able to prove that the story of his adventures is true.	☐	☐

The future

'"Very well," he said, "*I'll help* you."'

....

The Emperor of Blefuscu decided to help Gulliver **at the moment of speaking**.

We use the future tense with ***will*** to indicate an action that is decided at the time of speaking.

We also use the future tense with ***will*** to make predictions about the future.

Gulliver said: 'It**'ll be** a long journey, but I'm sure I can do it.'

(Gulliver predicts that the journey to England will be a long one.)

2 Grammar • **Make sentences with *will* using the verbs in the box. For each sentence, say if *will* indicates a Prediction (P) or a Decision made at the time of speaking (D).**

> destroy   make   punish   take   use   wear   write

1. ☐ One day, Gulliver saw a boat. 'I .... it to escape,' he thought.
2. ☐ 'I .... you to England,' agreed the captain.
3. ☐ Don't make the Emperor angry. He .... you.
4. ☐ 'I .... a book about Lilliput one day,' said Gulliver.
5. ☐ 'Come here, Gulliver. We .... you a new jacket,' said the women.
6. ☐ 'There's a terrible fire! The flames .... the palace!' shouted the Lilliputians.
7. ☐ 'It's cold today,' thought Gulliver. 'I .... my new jacket.'

3 Characters • Use 1-3 of the adjectives below to describe the characters in the story so far (you may use an adjective twice). Use a dictionary to help you with any words you don't know.

> changeable dangerous disbelieving friendly helpful
> likeable treacherous trustworthy ungrateful unselfish

1. The Emperor of Lilliput
2. The Emperor of Blefuscu
3. The important man who warns Gulliver
4. The ship's captain

4 Writing • Look at the sentences about how the Lilliputians write. Then choose two more things that you want to change in Lilliput, for example the laws, the treatment of poor people, the power of the Emperor. Write similar sentences explaining your ideas.

I want to change the way of writing because it is very inconvenient. It is easier to write from left to right or from right to left.

Chapter 5

THE TEXT AND BEYOND

1 Comprehension check • The statements about the story 1-8 are not correct. Correct them, giving a quotation from the story to prove you are right. There is an example.

0. Gulliver ~~easily forgot~~ didn't forget the problems in Lilliput and Blefuscu.
   I often thought about the two countries. I hoped they were not fighting again.
1. The sailors saw a small village near the beach.
2. The sailors sailed away fast because they were angry with Gulliver.
3. Gulliver was not afraid of the giants in the field.
4. The first giant wanted to hurt Gulliver by squeezing him in his fingers.
5. The farmer recognised that Gulliver was a man.
6. The farmer allowed his son to treat Gulliver badly.
7. The farmer's wife was angry when she saw the dead rat.
8. Grildrig means 'little nurse' in the language of Brobdingnag.

Comparatives

'There were two enormous rats... they were *as big as* dogs!'
'The giant was *as tall as* a church.'

We use *as* + adjective/adverb + *as* when we want to say that two people or things are similar.
'The corn was **much taller than** me.'

We use the comparative form of the adjective or adverb + *than* when we want to show the difference between two people or things.
One-syllable adjectives or adverbs add *-er*: **tall → taller**, **fast → faster**
We use **more** with adverbs ending in *-ly*: **quickly → more quickly**
We use **more** with three-syllable adjectives: **beautiful → more beautiful**
Two-syllable adjectives often have alternative comparative forms:
common → commoner OR **more common**
Some comparative forms are irregular: **good → better**, **bad → worse**

2 Grammar • Complete these sentences with *as* + adjective/adverb + *as*.

1. The sailors escaped .... they could. (*quickly*)
2. In Brobdingnag, Gulliver felt .... a Lilliputian. (*small*)
3. To the farmer's wife, he seemed .... an insect. (*disgusting*)
4. For Gulliver, the cat was .... a tiger. (*dangerous*)

3 Grammar • Now complete these sentences with the comparative adjective/adverb + *than*.

1. Everything in Brobdingnag is .... in a normal country. (*big*)
2. Glumdalclitch was .... her brother. (*kind*)
3. The baby was .... Gulliver. (*strong*)
4. Gulliver was .... the other sailors. (*adventurous*)
5. Gulliver had to speak .... he usually did. (*loudly*)
6. Gulliver thought that children behave .... adults. (*cruelly*)

4 Writing • Read the extract from Glumdalclitch's diary below.

> 7th June
>
> Today, Dad brought home a strange little man. At first Mum thought that he was a new kind of insect but now we have decided that he is a person like us. He has a lot of problems because of his size. My brother picked him up by his legs and the cat wanted to catch him. But he's very brave.

Now write two more diary entries by Glumdalclitch:

1. on the day after the attack by the rats
2. after she has begun to teach Gulliver

Chapter 6

THE TEXT AND BEYOND

1 Comprehension check • Who probably said or thought things like this?

1. 'You could make a lot of money.' ....
2. 'I don't think that Gulliver will like that.' ....
3. 'I feel sea-sick. I hope this journey ends soon.' ....
4. 'What a good idea! I'll be rich!' ....
5. 'I hate this life. How can I escape?' ....
6. 'I'm afraid that he will die.' ....
7. 'Nonsense! Let's continue to the next town.' ....
8. 'Go and bring the little man to me in the palace.' ....
9. 'Let's perform a special show.' ....

2 Vocabulary • Put the words about the theatre into the correct place in the table below.

> applaud   bow   clap   curtain   laugh   lights
> recite   rehearse   perform   scenery   stage   watch

What actors do	What people in the audience do	Theatre

3 Now, you perform! • Imagine Gulliver has returned to England and a journalist interviews him. Act out the interview with a partner. One of you asks these questions, the other one invents Gulliver's answers.

a Were you happy in the farmer's house?   **b** Why did the farmer decide to take you into town?   **c** Were your shows successful?   **d** Why didn't you enjoy performing?   **e** How did you feel when the Queen invited you to the palace?

4 Your opinion • **Do you agree or disagree with ideas 1-6? Why? Compare your answers with another person's.**

1. The farmer was wrong to show Gulliver to people for money.
2. Glumdalclitch was wrong to help with the money-making shows.
3. The people were wrong to laugh at Gulliver during the shows.
4. Gulliver was stupid not to enjoy taking part in the shows.
5. The farmer and Gulliver wanted to please the Queen for different reasons.
6. Chapter Six shows that money is a bad thing.

5 The story • **Read the text below and find seven differences from Jonathan Swift's story. There is an example.**

> The farmer decided to take Gulliver to different places and show him to the people for money. His son thought that this was a bad idea. They put Gulliver into a box on one of the horses. He had a very comfortable journey. At the first town, they stayed in a hotel and advertised the show in the newspaper. During the show, Gulliver laughed and clapped. Soon he became ill because he had to travel so much. This made the farmer sad. Finally, they came to the capital city. The show was very popular. One day, the Queen came to the show and told the farmer to bring Gulliver to the palace.

0. ~~His son~~ *His daughter* thought that this was a bad idea.

Chapter 7

THE TEXT AND BEYOND

1 Comprehension check • **Put these events into the correct order. The first has been done for you.**

a ☐ The dwarf puts Gulliver into a bone on the Queen's plate.
b ☐ The gardener's dog picks Gulliver up and carries him to the gardener.
c ☐ Wasps attack Gulliver.
d ☐ The dwarf puts Gulliver into a bowl of cream.
e ☐ An eagle flies away with Gulliver.
f ☐ The Queen and King order a special box for Gulliver.
g ☐ The dwarf shakes apples onto Gulliver's head.
h ☐ A monkey carries Gulliver onto the palace roof.
i ☐ A frog jumps into Gulliver's boat.
j ☐ 1 The Queen buys Gulliver from the farmer.

2A Vocabulary – animals • **Gulliver meets a lot of animals during his adventures. Can you find the eight hidden animals below?**

E	R	T	T	R	E	E	N	L
S	A	L	C	O	W	T	Z	E
E	T	F	A	T	T	G	O	L
E	R	R	T	O	T	S	I	L
J	M	O	N	K	E	Y	I	T
A	V	G	B	Y	A	L	T	B
Y	A	Z	D	O	G	A	R	U
R	F	O	X	U	L	O	D	W
R	S	S	H	E	E	P	M	Q

2B • **Answer these questions by giving the name of an animal from the puzzle.**

1. Which animals eat grass for a lot of the day?
2. Which animal sometimes spreads serious illness?
3. Which animal is an amphibian?
4. Which animal is known as 'man's best friend'?
5. Which animal is not liked by chicken farmers?

3 Vocabulary – accidents • Use one word from the box to fill each gap.

> died   drowned   fell   hit   hurt   rescued   sank   sting

6. Several times, Gulliver nearly ....
7. He nearly .... in the cream.
8. He nearly .... off the roof.
9. The wasps tried to .... him.
10. The hail stones .... him when they hit his body.
11. The boat nearly .... because of the frog.
12. The apples nearly .... him.
13. The ship's captain .... him.

4 Use your imagination • Gulliver met many large, dangerous animals in Brobdingnag. With a partner, imagine what happened when he came into contact with some of the things below. How did he escape from danger? Did anyone help him?

- a giant mosquito
- a garden pond
- a seagull
- a rainstorm with high winds
- fireworks
- robbers from another country of giants

Choose two or more of these dangers and write the story from Gulliver's point of view. Here is an example:

> Suddenly a giant mosquito appeared. It flew round me with a horrible sound. It wanted to suck all my blood out of my body. I attacked it with my sword. Luckily, Glumdalclitch saw us and came to send the mosquito away.

Chapter 8

THE TEXT AND BEYOND

1 Comprehension check • Answer the questions below.

1. Why did Gulliver separate from Captain Robinson?
2. Why did Gulliver look up and see the flying island?
3. What was strange about the eyes of the people on Laputa?
4. What was the decoration on the rich people's clothes?
5. Why did the people stop talking to Gulliver?
6. What was the name of the capital of Balnibarbi?
7. What was different about Lord Munodi's farm?
8. What did the people want when they came back from Laputa?

2 The story • Complete the table below to show some of the projects that Gulliver sees in the Academy.

	Description of the project	Purpose of the project
First project		
Second project		
Third project		

3 Vocabulary – maths • The people of Laputa like mathematics. Put the correct word from the box into the sentences below.

> divided by   degrees   even   minus   odd   plus   square root

a   2 .... 6 = 8
b   79 .... 6 = 73
c   84 .... 4 = 21
d   There are 180 .... in a triangle.
e   The .... of 16 = 4
f   1, 9 and 15 are all .... numbers.
g   4, 78 and 126 are all .... numbers.

94

4 Vocabulary – music • The people of Laputa also like music. Match the names of the instruments in the box with pictures 1-6.

a cello   **b** drums   **c** flute   **d** harp   **e** trombone   **f** violin

Find videos on the Internet of music played by some of the instruments. Then choose your six favourite instruments in order.

5 Writing • Gulliver visits many unusual imaginary lands. Use one of the ideas below or one of your own to write a shorty story about Gulliver in this new land.

- An underground land where nobody has ever seen life on the surface.
- A land where everybody has two heads – they are always arguing with themselves.
- An island which is made of gold and diamonds. The most valuable material in this land is normal stone.
- A land where there is no war.

Chapter 9

THE TEXT AND BEYOND

1 Comprehension check • **The statements about the story 1-8 are not correct. Correct them, giving a quotation from the story to prove you are right. There is an example.**

0. Gulliver ~~left~~ *didn't leave* Maldonado immediately.
   I spent a few days in the port of Maldonado...
1. Gulliver knew nothing about Glubbdubrib before he went there.
2. The Governor's servants disappeared and Gulliver never saw them again.
3. The Governor had a magician who controlled the ghosts.
4. All the heroes that Gulliver met had died a long time ago.
5. The heroes had a few good qualities.
6. Gulliver easily accepted that he had been wrong about his heroes.
7. The baby Struldbruggs look exactly like normal babies.
8. The Struldbruggs do not experience the problems of old age.

2 Gulliver's journey • **Gulliver's journey home will be a long one. Put the places below into the order in which he plans to visit them during the journey.**

☐ Japan   ☐ Luggnagg   ☐ Maldonado   ☐ Europe

3 The story • **Complete the chart below to show what the Struldbruggs are like.**

Before they are eighty	
At eighty	
After eighty	
At ninety	
At two hundred	

4 Heroes • **Choose any famous person from history. Write five questions which you would like to ask this person:**

Name of 'hero' ....

1. .... ?
2. .... ?
3. .... ?
4. .... ?
5. .... ?

Show your ideas to another person and discuss the possible answers.

5 Use your imagination • **The Struldbruggs are very strange. Imagine Gulliver's friend tells him about a new race of strange people. Use one of the ideas below or an idea you have created.**

- people who live from birth to death in nine years
- people who live backwards; they are born old and they die as babies
- people who turn into cats as soon as the sun sets and remain cats until sunrise

Now tell another person about your 'strange' people. Here are some questions to help you: What does the friend say about them? What are these people called? How do they live? What are their customs? Are they happy? Why/Why not?

6 Writing • **Write a diary entry written by the Governor after Gulliver's visit. Begin like this:**

> A young ship's doctor named Gulliver visited my island for a few days...

Chapter 10

THE TEXT AND BEYOND

1 Comprehension check • Eight of the statements about the story 1-10 are not correct. Correct them, giving a quotation from the story to prove you are right. There is an example.

0. Gulliver stopped in ~~Bermuda~~ *Barbados*.
   I decided to stop in Barbados.
1. All of the sailors on the *Adventure* died.
2. Gulliver saw villages but he didn't see any people in them.
3. The Yahoos ran away because Gulliver defended himself with his sword.
4. Gulliver was amazed first of all when the two horses talked to him.
5. The horses kept some Yahoos in one of the buildings.
6. The horses knew he wasn't a Yahoo because he wore clothes.
7. The horse believed what Gulliver told him about horses in England.
8. The horse decided there was no difference between human beings and Yahoos.
9. The master horse decided by himself that Gulliver must leave.
10. Gulliver has never forgotten his life with the Houyhnhnms.

2 Vocabulary • Write the words from the box in the correct column to describe the Houyhnhnms and Yahoos. Then find 4 pairs of opposites.

> clean   hard-working   intelligent   gentle   loud
> peaceful   fierce   rational   stupid   dirty   unattractive   violent

Houyhnhnms	Yahoos

98

3 The story • Gulliver makes some mistakes when he visits the land of the Houyhnhnms. Complete the sentences with the words from the box.

> angry   animals   believe   dislike   family   forty   missed
> people   pirates   sailors   sword   wars   Yahoos

1. When Gulliver found new ...., they were in fact ....
2. Gulliver attacked one of the .... with his .... and was surrounded by about .... creatures.
3. Gulliver expected to find .... in control of the country, not horses.
4. The horses didn't .... Gulliver's stories about his own country.
5. He made the horse .... when he explained about England's .... with its enemies.
6. He began to .... human beings. He was ashamed of being like the ....
7. In England, at first, Gulliver refused to meet his .... and he .... the Houyhnhnms.

4 Your reaction • Answer these questions about the story, giving your opinion.

1. What are the best qualities of the Houyhnhnms?
2. Do the Houyhnhnms act badly at any point?
3. Is Swift fair to human beings when he compares them to the Yahoos?
4. Would you like to visit the land of the Houyhnhnms?
5. Why did Swift choose horses to represent this noble type of beings?
6. Is Gulliver right to begin to dislike human beings?

5 Writing • Write a diary entry written by Don Pedro after he has met Gulliver. Begin like this:

> I have taken an English ship's doctor onto my ship.
> He has told me about....

EXTENSIVE LISTENING

1 Announcements • **Listen to the announcements and choose the correct answer to the questions.**

track 12

1. At what time will the rulers of Lilliput begin speaking?
   a two o'clock   **b** five o'clock   **c** half-past five   **d** three o'clock
2. What is the reason for changing the location of the performance?
   a rain   **b** snow   **c** cold weather   **d** high winds
3. What is the total reward for information about Gulliver?
   a £90 + £30   **b** £19 + £13   **c** £90 + £13   **d** £19 + £30
4. What flag is the pirate ship flying?
   a green with a yellow circle   **b** the traditional pirate flag   **c** green with an orange circle   **d** no flag
5. What do the professors believe the main advantage of their new plan is?
   a no tractors   **b** faster work   **c** fitter workers   **d** better fruit and vegetables

2 Is Gulliver a hero? • **Listen to the talk about Gulliver and answer the questions briefly. Base your answers on what the speaker says, not on your own opinions.**

track 13

1. Name three heroic qualities which Gulliver possesses.
   1 .... 2 .... 3 ....
2. Which special friendship does the speaker mention?
3. The speaker mentions two things which Gulliver never does. What are they?
4. Does Gulliver's behaviour when returns home seem 'heroic'? Why/Why not?
5. What does the story of the eagle illustrate about Gulliver's life?
6. What is the difference in the speaker's attitude to Gulliver in the first and second halves of the talk?

100

3 A dream • Listen to the conversation about a dream. For each question, choose the correct answer a, b, c or d.

track 14

1. The man dreamed about a place
   - a ☐ that was similar to Lilliput.
   - b ☐ that was ruled by an emperor.
   - c ☐ where the people were giants.
   - d ☐ where Gulliver was the king.

2. In the dream, he
   - a ☐ was reading *Gulliver's Travels*.
   - b ☐ stopped himself from sneezing.
   - c ☐ broke bridges and roads.
   - d ☐ soon made friends with the people.

3. In his dream, the people
   - a ☐ shot him with arrows.
   - b ☐ hurt him badly.
   - c ☐ were afraid of him.
   - d ☐ were angry with him.

4. In his dream, the little people
   - a ☐ helped him to fly back to his home.
   - b ☐ found a solution to the problem.
   - c ☐ remained angry with him.
   - d ☐ thought that he was an angel.

5. The other person thinks that he might dream about
   - a ☐ Lilliput again.
   - b ☐ giants who will be his friends.
   - c ☐ a situation that is the opposite of his first dream.
   - d ☐ the intelligent horses.

6. The man dreamed about these things because
   - a ☐ he had recently read *Gulliver's Travels*.
   - b ☐ he had recently read a similar book.
   - c ☐ he had a similar imagination to Jonathan Swift.
   - d ☐ he had liked the book very much.

SURF THE NET

Sumatra and Tasmania

Swift even included a map of Lilliput and Blefuscu in the book. According to the map, the imaginary islands are in the Pacific Ocean near the real country of Sumatra. He also said that Lilliput was near Tasmania, in Australia.

Use an Internet search engine to find information about these places and answer the questions.

1. Sumatra is a part of which large country?
2. What large endangered mammals live in Sumatra?
3. What are the three largest cities in Sumatra?
4. What disaster affected Sumatra in 2004?
5. In 1726 when Swift published his book, what was the name of Tasmania?
6. What is the approximate population of Tasmania?
7. What is its capital city?

Why do you think Swift chose this part of the world as a setting for Lilliput?

TRINITY • Preparation

1 GESE GRADE 5 – Festivals • In Lilliput, Gulliver sees dances and parades. Now think about your own country or town and answer the following questions.

   a Does your country have any festivals that a visitor might find interesting or strange? When do they take place? Can you find a picture and describe it to your class?

   b Have you ever been to a festival in another country or read about one on the Internet or in a magazine? For example, the Carnival in Rio. Describe the festival. Would you like to go to see it? Why?

2 GESE GRADE 5 – Entertainment • In Chapter 6, Gulliver becomes a 'spectacle for the people'. Answer the questions below.

   a Why do you think that he doesn't enjoy it?

   b Have you ever performed in front of a crowd either at school or somewhere else?

   c Do you remember if you enjoyed yourself or not?

   d Try to describe to your partner some of the things you were feeling before going on stage. Why might some people enjoy performing more than others?

3 GESE GRADE 6 – Travel • Here are some questions to help you talk to others about travel.

   a What is your favourite method of travel? Why do you like this method?

   b What has been your favourite journey in your life so far?

   c What places in the world do you want to visit in the future?

   d Do you prefer beach holidays or city tours or countryside holidays? Why?

   e Who do you like to travel with? Why?

   f In what ways might travelling make someone more independent and more open-minded?

PRELIMINARY • Preparation

1 READING PART 2 • Read the text below and choose the correct word for each space. For each question, write the correct letter a, b, c or d.

A VOYAGE TO LAPUTA AND BALNIBARBI

I was at home (**0**) ..*a*..... about ten days when a friend (**1**) .... mine came to see me. Captain Robinson (**2**) .... a ship called the *Hope-well*, and he wanted me to sail (**3**) .... him. At first I did not want to go, (**4**) .... he offered me a lot of money, and in the end I agreed. We sailed in the *Hope-well* to the East Indies. There was bad news when we arrived (**5**) .... The goods which Captain Robinson wanted (**6**) .... buy were not ready. 'I'll have to stay here and wait,' Captain Robinson (**7**) .... me. 'But you don't have to stay here with me, Gulliver. Let's buy a smaller ship, and you can go to the islands (**8**) .... here and buy and sell goods.' I agreed, and soon I was in command of a little ship of my own. (**9**) .... this little ship was attacked by pirates. They came (**10**) .... board, and they stole everything, including the ship itself.

0. **a** for	**b** in	**c** since	**d** by
1. **a** to	**b** with	**c** of	**d** and
2. **a** belonged	**b** owned	**c** did	**d** owning
3. **a** with	**b** by	**c** along	**d** on
4. **a** and	**b** instead	**c** although	**d** but
5. **a** here	**b** there	**c** their	**d** where
6. **a** for	**b** and	**c** to	**d** a
7. **a** told	**b** said	**c** explained	**d** asked
8. **a** far	**b** beyond	**c** by	**d** near
9. **a** Fortunately	**b** Happily	**c** Unfortunately	**d** Luckily
10. **a** at	**b** on	**c** to	**d** too

2 WRITING PART 2 • Imagine you are Gulliver. Write a card about your trip to the Academy in Lagado with Lord Munodi's friend. In your card, you should

- thank Lord Munodi's friend for taking you to the Academy
- say what you liked best
- ask if you could go back and see it again another day

Write your card in 35-45 words.

3 WRITING PART 1 • **Look at these sentences. For each question, complete the second sentence so that it means the same as the first. Use no more than three words.**

1. I asked the Emperor for permission to visit the capital city of Lilliput.
   I asked the Emperor if .... the capital city of Lilliput.
2. I could not enter the palace, of course, because I was too big.
   I wasn't .... to enter the palace, of course.
3. Some government ministers from Blefuscu invited me to visit their country.
   I .... visit Blefuscu by some of their government ministers.
4. There was a civil war in Lilliput, and many people were killed.
   The civil war .... in Lilliput.
5. 'May I go there?' I asked the Emperor.
   I asked the Emperor .... go there.

4 READING PART 3 • **Look at the statements below about the story. Decide if each statement is correct or incorrect. If it is correct, write A as your answer. If it is not correct, write B as your answer.**

		A	B
1.	Being a ship's doctor was Gulliver's first job.	☐	☐
2.	The Lilliputians tied Gulliver up while he was sleeping.	☐	☐
3.	The Emperor of Lilliput learnt Gulliver's language.	☐	☐
4.	Gulliver helped Lilliput in the war against Blefuscu.	☐	☐
5.	The Emperor and Gulliver agreed about how to end the war	☐	☐
6.	Gulliver saved the palace from a flood.	☐	☐
7.	Both Emperors were angry with Gulliver.	☐	☐
8.	When Gulliver arrived in Brobdingnag, the giants attacked him.	☐	☐
9.	Gulliver enjoyed all the time which he spent in Brobdingnag.	☐	☐
10.	Gulliver had proof which showed that his adventures were real.	☐	☐

PRELIMINARY • Preparation

5 READING PART 1 • Look at the text in each question. What does it say? Write the correct letter a, b or c. There is an example.

0

NOTICE
All eggs to be opened from the smaller end and not the bigger end

a ☐ All eggs must be opened from the smaller end.
b ☐ Eggs may be opened from either end.
c ☐ You should open your eggs from the smaller end.

1

BEWARE PIRATES
This area of the ocean is dangerous.
Please stay in port until the all clear is given.

a ☐ It is dangerous to stay in port.
b ☐ You must leave this dangerous area.
c ☐ It will be safe to cross this area later.

2

THE WORLD of GULLIVER'S TRAVELS
Enter the world of Jonathan Swift's marvellous book. Enjoy meeting our wild horses and exploring the miniature houses of Lilliput.

a ☐ This is an advertisement.
b ☐ This is a book review.
c ☐ This is an introduction to the book.

3

All students to attend mixed classes from 9 a.m. until 4 p.m. Lessons about family life for girls only until 5 p.m. Boys must do art at this time. Evening classes in art also available to all.

a ☐ Boys and girls study together for most of the time.
b ☐ Girls cannot study art.
c ☐ Boys can learn about family life.

4

REWARD
The giant, Gulliver, has fled to Blefuscu. £5,000 reward for information leading to his capture. Anyone assisting his escape will be put in prison.

a ☐ The reward is for anyone who catches Gulliver.
b ☐ The aim is to put Gulliver in prison.
c ☐ If you help Gulliver, you will be punished.

LET'S REVISE THE STORY

1 PICTURE SUMMARY • **Put the pictures from the story in the right order. Write a sentence under each one describing the scene.**

a

b

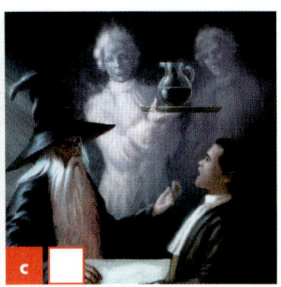
c

d

e

f

g

h

i

LET'S REVISE THE STORY

2 Comprehension check • Answer the questions below about Chapters 1-4, which take place in Lilliput and Blefuscu.

1. What is the full name of the person who tells the story (the narrator)?
2. Why was it a bad idea for Gulliver to sleep on the beach?
3. How did he communicate with the Lilliputians first of all? Later?
4. How did Gulliver defeat the forces of Blefuscu?
5. Gulliver saved the palace from fire. How did the Empress react?
6. Which children did not go to school in Lilliput?
7. What was the worst crime in Lilliput?
8. How did the Emperor want to punish Gulliver?

3 Comprehension check • Write the names of these things found in Chapters 5-9 of the story.

1. The name of Gulliver's ship on his second voyage: ....
2. The name of his best friend and helper in Brobdingnag: ....
3. The bird which carried Gulliver away from Brobdingnag: ....
4. The name of the flying island: ....
5. The two main interests of the people of this island: .... & ....
6. The meaning of the name Glubbdubrib: ....
7. The strange thing about the Governor's servants: ....
8. The special thing about the Struldbruggs: ....

4 Comprehension check • Answer the questions about Chapter 10 of the story.

1. Give three adjectives which describe the Yahoos.
2. Give three adjectives which describe the Houyhnhnms.
3. Give three adjectives which describe Gulliver after his return to England.

5 *Gulliver's Travels* and war • **There are several parts of the story which Swift uses to criticise war as stupid and irrational. For 1-8, say where the event occurred. Give more details.**

1. A ruler's soldiers march through a giant's legs.
2. Two groups of people fight a war for ridiculous reasons.
3. A ruler wants to continue fighting even though more people will die.
4. A ruler decides to punish Gulliver because he didn't help in a war.
5. The 'enemy' is more generous and friendly than Gulliver's original 'friend'.
6. A ruler doesn't want Gulliver to build big weapons.
7. Some great soldiers from the past were cruel.
8. Someone thinks that war proves that human beings are the worst creatures of all.

Do you think that Swift is right about war?

6 Review • **Write a short review of *Gulliver's Travels*. It should be suitable for a school or college magazine. Write 100-150 words. In your review, you should:**

- briefly write about the author and date of the original book
- briefly describe the story
- write about the main characters
- write about the main ideas of the story
- say what you most enjoyed and mention anything which you didn't like
- recommend the book for a suitable audience

7 Interview • **Imagine you are interviewing Gulliver for a newspaper. Write at least six questions and suitable answers. Begin like this:**

Interviewer: *Hello, Lemuel Gulliver. Our readers will be glad that you are safely back from your latest adventure. Where did you go this time?*

Gulliver: *I was in the land of the Houyhnhnms. They are a race of intelligent horses.*

Interviewer: *Horses! Can they speak? Do they belong to the people of that land?*

VALUES & FEELINGS

THINK!

1 During his voyages, Gulliver changes in character. Which words would you use to describe him at the beginning and end of his story?

Gulliver at the beginning
....

Gulliver at the end
....

active • energetic •
disappointed •
misanthropic •
optimistic • pessimistic

THE CHARACTERS

2 Use the words in the box to describe the characters below. Use a dictionary to check any unfamiliar words.

....
....
....

....
....
....

....
....
....

....
....
....

academic •
changeable •
friendly •
impractical •
intelligent •
kind-hearted •
logical • noble •
supportive •
unreliable • useless •
warlike

 **THE STORY**

3 In the word cloud you can see a list of feelings: which ones you can associate with *Gulliver's Travels*? Justify your ideas. For example: *The Emperor isn't grateful to Gulliver after he wins the War of the Eggs.*

Tradition Courage
Using power badly
Love
Ridiculous behaviour
Misunderstanding Intelligence
Stupidity Magic Greed for money
Disappointment
Mystery Science
Love of war Fear Determination
Experience Friendship
Lack of gratitude

 YOUR TURN!

4 Gulliver says humans are cruel and stupid, but let's disagree! List the good qualities of humans, e.g. *friendship, love, honesty*. Make your own word cloud using these qualities. Make them big or small according to the importance they have for you.

This reader uses the expansive reading approach: where reading is not only the enjoyment of the story and the discovery of a new language, but an opportunity to make cultural connections.

The new language introduced in this step of our **Reading & Training** series is listed below and language from lower steps is included too. For a complete list for all six steps, see *The Black Cat Graded Readers Handbook* at blackcat-cideb.com.

Step Three B1.2

Verb tenses
Present Perfect Simple: unfinished past with *for* or *since* (duration form)
Past Perfect Simple: narrative

Verb forms and patterns
Regular verbs and all irregular verbs in current English
Causative: *have / get* + object + past participle
Reported questions and orders with *ask* and *tell*

Modal verbs
Would: hypothesis
Would rather: preference
Should (present and future reference): moral obligation
Ought to (present and future reference): moral obligation
Used to: past habits and states

Types of clause
2nd Conditional: *if* + past, *would(n't)*
Zero, 1st and 2nd conditionals with *unless*
Non-defining relative clauses with *who* and *where*
Clauses of result: *so; so ... that; such ... that*
Clauses of concession: *although, though*

Other
Comparison: *(not) as / so ... as; (not) ... enough to; too ... to*

Step Three
If you enjoyed this reader, try another one in Step Three...

- *The Canterville Ghost,* by Oscar Wilde **(Life Skills)**
- *Three Men in a Boat,* by J.K. Jerome **(Life Skills)**
- *The Importance of Being Earnest,* by Oscar Wilde

Step Four
...or take a step forward to Step Four!

- *Beowulf*
- *Hamlet, Prince of Denmark,* by William Shakespeare
- *Northanger Abbey,* by Jane Austen